At Issue

Do Veterans Receive Adequate Health Care?

Other Books in the At Issue Series:

At Issue

Do Veterans Receive Adequate Health Care?

Lauri Harding, Book Editor

GREENHAVEN PRESS
A part of Gale, Cengage Learning

GALE
CENGAGE Learning

Detroit • New York • San Francisco • New Haven, Conn • Waterville, Maine • London

Christine Nasso, *Publisher*
Elizabeth Des Chenes, *Managing Editor*

For more information, contact:
Greenhaven Press
27500 Drake Rd.
Farmington Hills, MI 48331-3535
Or you can visit our Internet site at gale.cengage.com

LIBRARY OF CONGRESS CATALOGING-IN-PUBLICATION DATA

Do veterans receive adequate health care? / Lauri Harding, book editor.
    p. cm. -- (At issue)
Includes bibliographical references and index.
ISBN 978-0-7377-3916-9 (hardcover)
ISBN 978-0-7377-3917-6 (pbk.)
1. Veterans--Medical care--United States. 2. Terrorism--Government policy--United States--Juvenile literature. I. Harding, Lauri.
UB369.D6 2008
362.1086'970973--dc22
    2008013368

Printed in the United States of America
2 3 4 5 6 7 12 11 10 09 08

Contents

Introduction

Army Specialist Jeremy Duncan nearly bled to death from combat injuries in Iraq that left him with a fractured neck and mangled ear. All he wanted was to go home. After emergency life-saving care, he finally got his wish and was air-evacuated to Walter Reed Army Medical Center outside of Washington, D.C. Duncan thought his battles were over.

In truth, during his time at Walter Reed, Duncan continued to face considerable difficulties. He was assigned to Walter Reed's now-infamous "Building 18" for continued medical treatment. The dilapidated structure became the focus of media attention after a lengthy front-page article appeared in the *Washington Post* on February 18, 2007, describing deplorable conditions and inept staffing at the facility. *Post* staff writers Dana Priest and Anne Hull had visited Walter Reed's buildings over the course of several weeks and interviewed many patients. They wrote of mice droppings, stained carpeting, black mold showing through holes in the walls of Building 18, as well as "disengaged clerks, unqualified platoon sergeants, and overworked case managers." In the end, the unraveling scandal brought down several top military and civilian officials and appeared to symbolize the entire state of veterans' health care to the American public and the world.

Walter Reed had been the crown jewel among many military medical facilities spread throughout service branches and geographic localities. Taking its name from an army doctor who proved an association between mosquitoes and deadly yellow fever, the original facility was built in the early twentieth century on more than one hundred acres of valuable real estate in Washington. It first opened its doors in 1909 to receive ten patients. In 1951, its one hundred separate brick Georgian buildings became collectively known as the Walter Reed Army Medical Center. Over the years, the venerable institution was temporary home to the likes of former presidents Harry Truman and Ronald Reagan. Former president and military general Dwight D. Eisenhower died there in 1969, as did General Douglas MacArthur in 1964. Such distinguished world figures as Winston Churchill and King Hussein of Jordan had also been treated at Walter Reed. Touting its mission as the "Home of Warrior Care," the institution's system carried a staff of six thousand and treated 150,000 inpatients and outpatients at peak output.

In 2005, the federal Defense Base Realignment and Closure Commission announced the impending closure of Walter Reed, slated for 2010. Although insiders had known or anticipated this many years earlier, the finality of the decision likely contributed to the institution's decline, manifesting in human disengagement and uninterest in continued maintenance and improvement of the buildings. Additionally, five-plus years of sustained warfare in Afghanistan and Iraq resulted in an unending flow of casualties assigned there for care, pushing resources to their limits. This, in turn, created bureaucratic delays and backlogs in treatment appointments and day-to-day specialized needs. Many observers have noted, however, that even as the institution's services became more difficult to obtain, once medical care was received there, it was of a high quality.

The plan for Walter Reed involves moving staff members and services to the Naval Medical Center in Bethesda, Maryland, and creating a new, consolidated facility that will be named the Walter Reed National Military Medical Center (without army or navy designation). The current hospital has approximately 185 beds, but the contemplated consolidation would give the new facility about 340 beds. One-time costs are estimated at nearly $990 million, but with the new medical center in place, some estimate that the Pentagon will save $301 million over the next twenty years. The plan will provide the opportunity to build a state-of-the-art single facility that more efficiently serves all military services in one place. The old facility will remain open and continue with services until the transition is complete.

As for Army Specialist Jeremy Duncan, he and others were called to testify before a subcommittee of the U.S. House of Representatives Committee on Oversight and Government Reform about personal experiences with the military health care system. He told subcommittee members that living conditions at Walter Reed varied greatly for outpatient soldiers (which he became), according to the particular building assigned. Building 18 was clearly "the ghetto," he opined, but it had good television and video games. He was moved to the nicer Building 14, but that building had neither television nor video games. As of September 2007, Duncan was transferred to Fort Campbell, Kentucky, and was working to rejoin his unit overseas in Iraq.

1

America's Military Has Broken Its Promise to Veterans for Lifetime Health Care

Henry Mark Holzer

Henry Mark Holzer is professor emeritus at Brooklyn Law School in New York. He is also a practicing appellate lawyer who specializes in constitutional law.

World War II (WWII) and Korean War–era veterans serving in combat received low pay for their hazardous-duty service. Military recruiters compensated by offering free lifetime health care for veterans with twenty years of service. For decades, the government lived up to its promise. But in 1996, the Bill Clinton administration, anxious to reduce its budget, broke that promise and made veterans purchase Medicare plans. Retired veterans filed a class-action lawsuit and won their case on initial appeal. However, when the government appealed for an en banc review (with all appellate judges participating, and not just a three-judge panel), the veterans lost. The initial three-member panel decision was the correct one. These veterans honorably fulfilled their end of the bargain and the U.S. government needs to do the same.

The Canadian poet Robert W. Service wrote in his *The Cremation of Sam McGee*, "A promise made is a debt unpaid." To that I would add: A debt unpaid is an ongoing moral obligation. All the more so when it is the government that breached a promise to its veterans.

From the early days of World War II and all through the Korean War, our government desperately needed men who were committed to military service. To get them, the services sent out the word to their worldwide recruiters: Offer a deal to every eligible civilian, and to every soldier, sailor, airman and marine: *Serve 20 years honorably, and when you retire, the government will provide free lifetime medical care for you and your dependents. Serve your country, and it will care for you and yours.*

No fine print, no equivocations, no catches, no lawyer-like parsing of words.

Thousands upon thousands of American men accepted the government's offer and performed their end of the bargain. One was William Schism, a 36-year veteran of World War II, Korea, and Vietnam. Another was Robert Reinlie . . . , a 25-year vet, who survived more than thirty bombing missions over Europe and later served in Korea and Vietnam. Today, Schism, Reinlie, and countless other veterans of World War II and Korea, are fighting another battle—not against the Axis Powers but, ironically, against their own government.

The Clintonistas reneged on our Nation's solemn promise of free lifetime medical benefits to the men who served and fought for their country in time of war.

A Promise Broken

For years, the government lived up to its promise to our World War II and Korean veterans. Until Bill Clinton. As George Washington Law School professor Jonathan Turley has written recently, "[I]n 1995 the Clinton Administration was looking for things to cut out of a budget to fund greater priorities, like politically popular subsidies and transportation projects." So, to help tobacco farmers, to build even more bridges in Robert Byrd's West Virginia, and to fund similar boondoggles, the Clintonistas reneged on our Nation's solemn promise of free lifetime medical benefits to the men who served and fought for their country in time of war. Henceforth, all World War II and Korean vets over age 65 (virtually all of them) would have to rely on Medicare—which, because of the premiums, deductibles, and co-pay requirements, is not "free." Many of the veterans, now in their 80s and 90s, cannot afford these payments. Nor was it economically feasible for any of them to sue the government in an effort to enforce their rights.

Not until a champion appeared in the person of retired Air Force Colonel George E. ("Bud") Day. A veteran of World War II, Korea, and Vietnam, Col. Day is the only American to have escaped from North Vietnam into South Vietnam. Recaptured after ten horrific days on the run, Bud Day would spend 67 months as a POW [prisoner of war] in the infamous Hanoi Hilton [the ironic name given to a brutal prison camp], and would return to the United States to become the most decorated living American. Col. Day wears the highest medal our country can award: the Medal of Honor. . . .

Bud is also a lawyer. In the late 1990s, on behalf of Schism, Reinlie, and the uncountable veterans who had fulfilled their part of the bargain with the US government, Col. Day commenced a class action under a federal statute called the Little Tucker Act. Bud's theory was straightforward. Military recruiters had offered free lifetime medical care in return for 20 years' service. The veterans had accepted that offer by serving a minimum of 20 years. The government, by forcing the vets into Medicare, had breached its contract. Thus, the veterans were entitled to the promised medical care, and to damages.

Faulty Reasoning

The government's first line of defense was to deny that their military recruiters had made any such promises. But in the face of incontrovertible evidence to the contrary, the Department of Justice lawyers backed off, resorting to a fall-back position: Sure, okay, the promises were made, *but our recruiters had no legal authority to make them.*

This argument was patent nonsense. It defies common sense that thousands of recruiters, worldwide, wholly on their own and with no directives from the top, came up with a "free lifetime medical care" ploy in order to lure men into a 20-year hitch.

The trial judge bought the argument and threw the veterans out of court. Col. Day appealed, and a three-judge panel of the United States Court of Appeals for the Federal Circuit reversed the lower court, holding that the promises *were* authorized; that the government *had* breached its contract. Now on the defensive, the Department of Justice asked *all* the court's active judges to rehear the case in an *en banc* review. Because of the importance of the issue, the court agreed.

By then, I was acquainted with Col. Day, who had just contributed the introduction to *"Aid and Comfort": Jane Fonda in North Vietnam,* a book I co-wrote with my wife, Erika Holzer. When I learned about Bud's class action lawsuit, I volunteered to help—being a veteran myself, and having specialized for over forty years in appellate law.

Even if we were to prevail in the Supreme Court two years hence, too many veterans will have already gone to their graves bearing a sense of betrayal, believing that their last battle had been a lost cause.

A Disappointing Conclusion

Col. Day forcefully argued the case in early March of [2002] to a packed courtroom—veterans from all over the country had made the pilgrimage to Washington, DC. [In November 2002], the Federal Circuit rendered its decision. The veterans lost. The 9-4 majority ruled that, yes, the recruiters had indeed made the promises "in good faith," and yes, the veterans—those who had managed to live through World War II and Korea—had fulfilled their part of the bargain by serving their country for at least 20 years. *But because nowhere in our vast government hierarchy—neither in the Executive Branch nor in the Congress—could any statute, regulation, or other power be found that allowed military recruiters to fill their quotas by promising medical benefits, there was no contract to breach.*

The Court of Appeals was wrong. There *was* authority—in the President of the United States in his capacity as Commander-in-Chief, as well as under at least one federal statute. Accordingly, Col. Day and I will seek review in the Supreme Court of the United States.

But review, being discretionary, is difficult to obtain. And even were we to succeed in invoking the Supreme Court's jurisdiction, the case would not be decided until sometime in 2004—at least two years from now. By then, according to the Department of Veterans Affairs estimate, nearly *one million* veterans of the Greatest Generation will have died; they are dying at the rate of 1,200 men a day.

Even if we were to prevail in the Supreme Court two years hence, too many veterans will have already gone to their graves bearing a tragic sense of betrayal, believing that their last battle had been a lost cause. [The U.S. Supreme Court denied review, letting stand the federal circuit court's decision.]

2

Only Congress Has the Authority to Make Promises for Lifetime Benefits

Paul R. Michel

Paul R. Michel was appointed to the U.S. Court of Appeals for the Federal Circuit in 1988. He became chief judge of the court in 2004. The U.S. Court of Appeals for the Federal Circuit is one of thirteen appellate courts. The Court of Appeals for the Federal Circuit has national jurisdiction to hear appeals in specialized cases, while the twelve regional courts, located across the nation, primarily hear appeals from district courts within their circuit. Decisions from these circuit courts of appeals can be overruled—vacated, reversed, or modified—only by the U.S. Supreme Court. In this particular case, the Supreme Court denied review, in effect letting stand the appellate court's decision.

It is not denied that many military recruiters, to encourage enlistments, did indeed make oral promises of free lifetime medical care to recruits. But the question before the Court is whether they had the authority to make those promises. For the reasons discussed in the full opinion, the Court finds that only Congress has the power to offer such benefits. Nothing in any act of Congress ever authorized free lifetime health care for all retired veterans; neither did Congress later ratify the acts of military recruiters who offered such benefits, even though offered in good faith. Americans are sympathetic, but the constitutional principle of "balance of power" dictates that relief must come from Congress and not the courts.

Paul R. Michel, Opinion for the U.S. Court of Appeals for the Federal Circuit, *Schism v. United States*, 316 F.3d 1259, Court of Appeals for the Federal Circuit, 2002.

To induce people to join the armed services during the World War II and Korean War era and make it a career, military recruiters, under the direction of superiors, orally promised recruits that if they served on active duty for at least 20 years, they would receive free lifetime medical care for themselves and their dependents. The government concedes such promises were made in good faith and relied upon. Plaintiffs allege that they were fulfilled until 1995 when, plaintiffs assert, the government breached these implied-in-fact contracts by effectively denying them free care so they had to purchase Medicare Part B insurance in order to be treated by civilian doctors or obtain medications without paying fees because space was no longer available in military facilities where care and medications were free. We must decide whether the government is bound by those promises. . . .

Events Leading Up to the Dispute

The essential facts in this case are undisputed. . . .

[Plaintiffs/appellants William O.] Schism and [Robert L.] Reinlie each accumulated 20 years of active duty in the Armed Services. Schism enlisted in the United States Navy in April 1943, and was honorably discharged in February 1946. In 1951, he received an indefinite appointment in the Air Force. In 1956, he began active service, which continued until his retirement in 1979. Thus, his Air Force service alone entitled him to retirement benefits.

Reinlie enlisted in the United States Army in 1942 and served on active duty until October 1945. He entered the Air Force in 1951 and, in 1953, he received an indefinite term appointment. Reinlie served continuously until he retired from the Air Force in 1967. While the precise dates of Reinlie's service are not in the record before us, he apparently had sufficient retirement credits between his World War II service and his subsequent Air Force service to total 20 years. The government has indicated that the relevant start of service dates for plaintiffs are 1951 for Schism and 1953 for Reinlie, the dates of their indefinite appointments. The retirees do not dispute this fact, so we deem these to be the relevant dates. Therefore, the only promises that matter are those of the Air Force recruiters in 1951 and 1953.

At the time the retirees joined the Air Force, recruiters allegedly promised free lifetime medical care for them and their dependents in exchange for serving 20 years. Plaintiffs contend that their acceptance of this offer and the government's subsequent practice of providing free medical care formed an implied-in-fact contract. In 1995, however, the government implemented TRICARE, a program that essentially modeled the availability of health care benefits for retirees along the lines of a health maintenance organization ("HMO"). Retired service members who qualify for Medicare under the Social Security Act, however, are not eligible for TRICARE benefits. But TRICARE does allow military retirees over age 65 to maintain the military health coverage that they had previously received for free by paying a monthly Medicare fee, which is deducted from their social security benefit payments. On December 11, 1996, plaintiffs brought a Little Tucker Act action [a type of legal claim] alleging that the government had breached its implied-in-fact contracts by requiring them to pay for Medicare coverage.

Judicial Address

Before the district court, the retirees sought "an order requiring the United States to cease deducting payments from their retired pay and to provide [them] and their dependents the unlimited free medical care for which they allegedly contracted." The retirees argued that the recruiters' authority to make promises of full free lifetime medical care had multiple sources, the clearest being the broad language of 5 U.S.C. § 301 (1958). Under that and other statutes, the military departments promulgated for decades regulations that governed the eligibility of retirees for health care, including Army Regulation AR 40-505 ¶2(b)(2) (1934) (allowing use of Army hospitals to Army retirees "provided sufficient accommodations are available for their treatment"), Army Regulation AR 40-590 ¶6(b)(1) (1935) (limiting availability of care from Army hospitals to "retired personnel on inactive status" who will benefit "by hospitalization for a reasonable time," not those who "merely" require "domiciliary care by reason of age or chronic invalidism"), and Air Force Regulation AFR 160-73 ¶14(h) (1951) (limiting hospitalization of retired Air Force personnel to those "who will be benefited by hospitalization for a reasonable length of time"). In addition, the 1943 edition of the Navy's Manual of the Medical Department ("MEDMAN") also states: "Retired officers and enlisted men, inactive, are not entitled to civilian medical and hospital treatment at government expense. They are entitled to treatment in naval hospitals by naval medical officers when available upon application. . . ." Plaintiffs cite and rely on all these sources.

In further support for their position, the retirees pointed to a 1945 letter written by James Forrestal, then-Secretary of the Navy, to "Naval Reserve and Temporary USN Officers." The letter encourages reserve officers to transfer to the Regular service. Attached to this letter was a recruitment brochure indicating that retired Navy personnel would receive free medical care. The retirees asserted that this letter explicitly authorized the recruiters' oral promises of free lifetime health care. In a similar vein, they contended that because Congress later expressly authorized certain plans for some retired service members and their dependents, e.g., "CHAMPUS" (Civilian Health and Medical Program of the United States), 10 U.S.C. § 1086 (1966), it also necessarily authorized recruiters' earlier oral promises of free lifetime medical care. Citing the repeated appropriations of funds then used to pay for military medical care, including the care given to retirees, Schism alternatively argued that Congress later ratified the recruiters' promises.

The government responded that none of the military services' regulations in place before 1956 promised free unconditional lifetime medical care for retirees and, moreover, that 5 U.S.C. § 301 did not authorize promises of such care even if the regulations did conditionally authorize care under certain circumstances. Further, the government argued, Congress did not ratify the recruiters' oral promises because it never explicitly appropriated funds for an entitlement to free lifetime medical care for retirees.

Initial Rejection

On August 31, 1998, the district court rejected the retirees' claim, holding that as a matter of law neither the relevant statutes nor the regulations authorized the recruiters' promises of full free lifetime medical care. In reaching this conclusion, the court explained that while "recruiters made promises to potential recruits that they could obtain lifetime medical care for themselves and their dependents by joining the armed forces and fulfilling certain service obligations," those promises conflicted with the regulations then in place. Accordingly, the court concluded, because the recruiters lacked the requisite authority to make promises binding on the government, no valid contracts between the retirees and the relevant service branches were formed. Summary judgment was therefore granted in favor of the government.

Temporary Respite

On February 8, 2001, a panel of this court reversed, stating "[t]here is nothing in the regulations or law prior to 1956 that would have prohibited recruiters from making [the promises of full free lifetime medical care]; indeed those regulations appear to authorize them. At the least, there is no inconsistency between them." The full court then granted the government's petition for a rehearing *en banc* [with all judges of a court hearing the case] and, by order dated June 13, 2001, asked the parties to rebrief the appeal, addressing (among other things) the following issues: (1) whether promises of free medical care for life are enforceable in general and in particular under 5 U.S.C. § 301; (2) whether congressional appropriations had ratified those promises; and (3) the relevance, if any, of the new TRICARE for Life Bill, enacted in December 2000, Pub. L. No. 106-398, § 712 (2000), the conference report of which states that it "provides permanent lifetime TRICARE eligibility for Medicare-eligible military retirees and their families beginning in fiscal year 2002" [*Congressional Record*, October 11, 2000].

On appeal, the retirees contend "the government forced [them] to go on Medicare and pay for their own medical care." Citing the "unavailability of care under Medicare," the retirees explained that they had to pay for Medicare Part B and supplemental insurance. Asserting that paying these fees violated their contract with the government, the retirees are seeking damages. While the nature and extent of these damages are not explained in detail in the briefs, the logical conclusion is that the retirees seek the costs they allegedly have been "forced" to pay "to get less medical care than they were receiving at no cost before [the alleged breach]." Indeed, these are the only damages that the retirees discuss in any detail. . . .

Benefits for retired military personnel—and for civilian retired federal employees, for that matter—depend upon an exercise of legislative grace, not upon principles of contract, property, or 'takings' law.

A History of Legislative Oversight

Benefits for retired military personnel—and for civilian retired federal employees, for that matter—depend upon an exercise of legislative grace, not upon principles of contract, property, or "takings" law. . . .

Congress has since 1884 repeatedly exercised its authority by enacting statutes that defined the breadth of health care authorized for members of the military and their dependents. . . .

In 1956, Congress began a series of legislative acts that have formed the basis for modern-day retired military medical care. The three-fold purpose of the medical care program for retirees is best explained by the Department of Defense:

> To provide incentives for armed forces personnel to undertake military service and remain in that service for a full career; to help ensure the availability of physically acceptable and experienced personnel in time of national emergency; and to provide military physicians and dentists exposure to the total spectrum of demographically diverse morbidity necessary to support professional training programs and ensure professional satisfaction for a medical service career. . . .

A mere ten years later, in 1966, Congress revisited the issue of retiree medical care when it amended the provisions of Title 10 dealing with health care for (among others) retirees and their dependents. In so doing, Congress granted the authority to the Department of Defense to contract for the provision of civilian health care for these groups (resulting in the Civilian Health and Medical Program for the Uniformed Services—CHAMPUS). . . .

Because the very program Congress enacted in part for the retirees' benefit was never 'free,' it is clear that Congress never intended health care for retired career personnel to be without cost to the retirees.

CHAMPUS guaranteed retirees who were not yet entitled to Medicare benefits access to authorized health services from civilian sources as an alternative to care from military facilities. Of significance is that CHAMPUS was not a "free" program. . . .

Never Free

Thus, because the very program Congress enacted in part for the retirees' benefit was never "free," it is clear that Congress never intended health care for retired career personnel to be without cost to the retirees.

Following yet another examination of health care for retirees, in 1986, Congress enacted 10 U.S.C. §§1097, 1099 to further improve the health care system for service members. This legislation provided the authority for the military's eventual implementation of TRICARE in the early 1990s, which offered CHAMPUS-eligible beneficiaries (retirees under 65 years of age) a choice among a health maintenance organization-type program, a preferred provider network program, and CHAMPUS benefits. . . .

Most recently, of course, Congress exercised its authority over health care for retired military members by introducing TRICARE For Life, which provides a pharmacy services program for Medicare-eligible beneficiaries and authorizes Medicare-eligible beneficiaries who enroll in Medicare Part B to participate in CHAMPUS.

While Congress has legislated extensively in the realm of military health care, as the history above indicates, not once has it statutorily authorized the secretaries of the military departments to contract with recruits for health benefit entitlements. . . .

One cannot reasonably infer that by empowering service secretaries to run their respective departments, Congress was silently authorizing them to grant health care benefits via oral promises to recruits by the service's recruiters.

Of course, had Congress legislated that the military secretaries could contract with recruits for specific health care benefits, the situation would be different. However, because Congress (1) has enacted statutes for over 100 years that govern the level and availability of health care benefits for active and retired members of the armed services and their dependents; and (2) has never provided funds for contracts made by the secretary with recruits to grant health care, the inescapable conclusion is that Congress simply did not intend to delegate its authority over health care benefits for military members. Rather, it intended to occupy the entire field. In that context, one cannot reasonably infer that by empowering service secretaries to run their respective departments, Congress was silently authorizing them to grant health care benefits via oral promises to recruits by the service's recruiters. . . .

We note at the outset that the retirees' implied-in-fact contract argument fails to take into account their written enlistment agreements.

Why the Argument Fails

We note at the outset that the retirees' implied-in-fact contract argument fails to take into account their written enlistment agreements. It is well settled that the existence of an express contract precludes the existence of an implied-in-fact contract dealing with the same subject matter, unless the implied contract is entirely unrelated to the express contract. . . .

Reinlie and Schism agreed in an express, written contract to be bound by military regulations and statutes. Those regulations and statutes expressly address health care for military retirees, and provide expressly that retirees and their dependents were not entitled to full free lifetime medical care. Accordingly, the retirees' contract claim is foreclosed because [as stated in the 1997 decision *Trauma Servs. Group v. United States*] an "implied-in-fact contract cannot exist if an express contract already covers the same subject matter." . . .

No Authority

The plaintiffs also assert that the Commander-in-Chief's inherent power in combination with 10 U.S.C. §§ 3013, 5013, and 8013—which authorize the positions and enumerate the duties of the Secretaries of the Army, Navy, and Air Force respectively—authorized the recruiters' promises. . . .

As Commander-in-Chief, the President does not have the constitutional authority to make promises about entitlements for life to military personnel that bind the government because such powers would encroach on Congress' constitutional prerogative to appropriate funding. Under Article I, § 8, only Congress has the power of the purse. . . .

Nor may he obligate funds for future years for an activity unless it has been authorized by law. Thus, to the extent that military recruiters, in the absence of statutory authority, make promises that impose an obligation on the federal Treasury, they exceed their constitutional authority and abrogate Congress' authority under the Appropriations Clause, U.S. Const., art. I, § 9, cl. 7. . . .

No Ratification or Acquiescence

Because we hold [that] neither 5 U.S.C. § 301, nor any other asserted authority, authorizes the recruiters' promises of free lifetime medical care, the retirees can prevail only if the promises were later ratified by Congress. We hold that Congress did not ratify them.

Ratification is "the affirmance by a person of a prior act which did not bind him but which was done or professedly done on his account, whereby the act, as to some or all persons, is given effect as if originally authorized by him" [according to the Restatement (Second) of Agency § 82 (1958)]. . . .

The relevant question is whether Congress acquiesced in the military departments' interpretation of the statutes and regulations so as to provide the requisite "actual authority" to contract for an entitlement to free lifetime medical care for retired personnel. . . .

The doctrine of acquiescence is premised upon Congress' failure to act in response to an action it might view as previously unauthorized, unlike the ratification context where Congress affirmatively acted to demonstrate its approval of an agency action. . . .

[When] Congress considered healthcare for retirees it acted decisively by denying entitlement to free lifetime medical care. Thus, Congress' action itself vitiates any argument of acquiescence. . . .

In the end, because no actual authority existed for the recruiters' promises of full free lifetime medical care, the plaintiffs cannot show a valid implied-in-fact-contract. Thus, plaintiffs' claim must fail as a matter of law. . . .

We cannot readily imagine more sympathetic plaintiffs than the retired officers of the World War II and Korean War era involved in this case.

The plaintiffs correctly argue this legislation does not alter their breach of contract claim against the government. But while it does not alter their claim, the TRICARE For Life provision does further demonstrate that Congress did not believe retirees had an unqualified right to free lifetime medical care. TRICARE For Life was heralded as a breakthrough for retirees over the age of 65 and their dependents. . . .

If Congress believed that the veterans already had free lifetime healthcare, why would such a program be needed? . . . The question answers itself: Congress never thought that it had given military retirees the right to free lifetime medical care, and nor did it believe that it had vested the various military branches with the power to make binding promises to that effect. . . .

Only Sympathy Is Offered

We cannot readily imagine more sympathetic plaintiffs than the retired officers of the World War II and Korean War era involved in this case. They served their country for at least 20 years with the understanding that when they retired they and their dependents would receive full free health care for life. The promise of such health care was made in good faith and relied upon. Again, however, because no authority existed to make such promises in the first place, and because Congress has never ratified or acquiesced to this promise, we have no alternative but to uphold the judgment against the retirees' breach-of-contract claim.

Federal judges have a duty to uphold the Constitution and the laws, even if that means making unpleasant or unpopular decisions.

Federal judges have a duty to uphold the Constitution and the laws, even if that means making unpleasant or unpopular decisions. Congress, on the other hand, has the power to make law, not simply to interpret and apply it. . . .

Perhaps Congress will consider using its legal power to address the moral claims raised by Schism and Reinlie on their own behalf, and indirectly for other affected retirees.

For the reasons stated above, the district court's grant of summary judgment for the government is affirmed.

3

The TRICARE System of Health Care for Veterans Is Unsatisfactory

The Military Retiree Grass Roots Group

The Military Retiree Grass Roots Group is an informal group of individuals with the common goal of regaining lifetime medical care benefits for veterans, benefits that they argue were promised to them. The group's members act together to lobby Congress and engage the media to keep attention focused on their issues.

Military personnel are the only federal employees without a funded health care insurance plan. Instead, they must use a government-run managed health care program called TRICARE. The program is inferior to parallel programs for retirees in the public and private sectors. Persistent problems with choice, cost, provider access, quality, and reliability plague the system. Putting more money into TRICARE is not the answer: the system is controlled by for-profit private contractors whose gross profit margin is staggering. It is unjust that government civilian employees have a better health care system than those whose lives are on the line defending them.

Military personnel under age 65, both active and retired, are the only federal employees whose families have no funded entitlement to health care and no health insurance. Instead of an insurance program with choice such as that offered other federal employees, they are forced into an expen-

The Military Retiree Grass Roots Group, "The White Paper," *The Retired Military Advocate*, May 20, 2002. Reproduced by permission. http://mrgrg-ms.org/white-paper-20-may-2002.html.

sive, contractor-run, new government managed care program entitled TRICARE. Many consider TRICARE unsatisfactory.

The American public . . . believes generally that military personnel have good, free health care upon entering service through retirement.

Promises made to career military personnel concerning health care are well-documented in official publications and brochures. The promises were even published on annual statements of military compensation. Those promises have been broken repeatedly. The American public is not aware of this fact, and believes generally that military personnel have good, free health care upon entering service through retirement. This is patently false. The violations of promises to career military personnel are already the subject of several lawsuits.

Retired military pay, survivor benefits, compensation for service-connected disabilities, and health care are all *inferior* to comparable federal civilian programs and grades. . . .

Not an Improvement

The Department of Defense [DOD] was directed in the early 1990's to develop and implement a health care program along the lines of the nationalized health care system that the nation had rejected. The new system replaced a non-profit system called CHAMPUS [Civilian Health and Medical Program of the United States] with a for-profit system called TRICARE. The rationale was based solely on reducing cost to the government. Instead, overall cost to the government and TRICARE beneficiaries increased.

The "reduction" in government cost was accomplished by simply "shifting" the expense to generations of those who had already completed a lifetime of service to the nation in the armed forces. At the same time, the amount of health care that could be purchased with remaining government funds was decreased by the new requirement to pay for massive profits to contractors that now determine nearly every aspect of health care for military families, and for a burgeoning civilian bureaucracy to manage the new government program. . . .

Profit Mongering

In circumstances driven solely by capitalistic goals, it may be appropriate to focus first on cost reduction. However, we believe the government made a major strategic error in applying that principle to health care for the armed forces and their families, upon whom our national defense rests. Military families and uniformed members of the military consider the level of health care provided as the *most* fundamental indicator of the government's commitment to care for them in return for their sacrifice of life and limbs, and their families' welfare, for the good of the nation.

The simple fact that government's own civilian employees have better health care than its uniformed military members and families is sufficient evidence, all other assertions to the contrary notwithstanding, that the TRICARE experiment has failed. DOD is not providing the health care military families earn(ed) for military retirees under 65 years of age.

We have seen no evidence to demonstrate that TRICARE was even successful in its primary goal of cost reduction, although we know service has declined significantly. . . . We also know that, regardless of any government cost reduction, costs have risen for the beneficiary, with the difference being channeled to contractor profits.

Individual beneficiaries whose compensation had already eroded significantly, now find they have neither the pay nor the promised health care. Instead, they find they are faced with denial of care, harassment, and major uncompensated out-of-pocket costs. For example, TRICARE Dental, probably one of the worst plans in the nation, is paid completely by beneficiaries and includes absolutely no government funding.

That further increases out of pocket medical expenses for military people whose pay was never intended to include substantial health care costs.

The overall impact of TRICARE on many military families, both active and retired, is a deep sense of betrayal.

Palpable and Impalpable Impact

The overall impact of TRICARE on many military families, both active and retired, is a deep sense of betrayal not understood by their past and present senior leaders, who continue to experience preferential VIP [very important person] treatment for themselves and have no personal experience with TRICARE. Their decisions are based upon advice from career civilian operators of the TRICARE program, whose jobs (and profits) depend on perpetuation and maintenance of the status quo.

As a consequence, some military families choose not to reenlist. Many retired members now advise potential career soldiers, and their own families, not to join or remain in the armed forces past their initial service obligations. We have documented cases of young active duty families turning to MEDICAID to fill gaps in health care for their small children. It is not likely these soldiers will become candidates for careers in the military. The White Paper [from which this viewpoint is excerpted] provides thoroughly documented cases of patient abuse with references to over 400 cases involving both active and retired families.

Because of the negative consequences of TRICARE on service members and their families, and on the nation's security, the military health care system must be restored to its former preeminence. As a minimum, we wish to restore military health care to a standard that families can afford.

Easy but Shallow Fix

What unpopular wars and generational differences could not achieve, BRAC [Base Realignment and Closure] and the concurrent implementation of TRICARE accomplished "overnight." Many military retirees and families became isolated from the larger military family to which they always belonged. Now, they feel welcome neither at military facilities nor in the civilian community health facilities that see TRICARE as an albatross—one that increases administrative costs while failing to reimburse for even their costs of providing care.

Even the entire TRICARE coding system is unique, yet DOD acts arrogantly as if they expect all physicians to maintain two sets of books—one for the majority of the nation using MEDICARE, and another only for military families forced into TRICARE.

The new TRICARE bureaucracy siphoned off active duty personnel from direct care, and created new civil service positions to plug holes in this budding but hemorrhaging new health care system. Each TRICARE region became a two star command, each with a different structure, guaranteeing more administrators, with less direct care. As regional differences became apparent, with contracts different for each contractor, rules regarding beneficiary allowances and disallowances became bizarre. Example: A wife and daughter in the same state having surgery in the same month could not receive identically prescribed medications for pain from the same authorized TRICARE Pharmacy chain.

As TRICARE problems mounted, the government approach has been to provide more money, not to solve the basic problem.

Many people believe that DOD's military health care problems should have been solved in the first place by moving to the existing FEHBP [Federal Employee's Health Benefit Plan] program used for all other federal employees, with an increased subsidy (90%) and pharmacy benefit in recognition of the additional sacrifices of military families throughout their careers. . . .

What the Numbers Do Not Show

Those who are satisfied with TRICARE are primarily the 85% of the active duty population in good health and using the TRICARE Prime HMO [health maintenance organization], where DOD places its funds and emphasis. Those most dissatisfied are families on TRICARE Standard, which includes about half the DOD eligible population of 8.8 million, and mostly retiree families.

In the opinions of many, the TRICARE system is currently so expensive to the government and to users compared to other options available, and provides such poor responsiveness and care for associated funding, that only a wholesale replacement of the system will solve the problems. The entire TRICARE system demands the urgent attention of a GAO [Government Accountability Office] audit to define the TRICARE "bloat."

TRICARE is a very complex and contradictory for-profit experiment that has broken promises and dashed expectations of the nation's professional volunteer soldiers and their families.

However, in the long-term interest of providing the best quality health care at the lowest cost to military families, benchmark legislation . . . needs to be enacted by the Congress that reaffirms the commitment to lifetime health care in return for the solemn obligations undertaken and met by those who risk their lives for the nation expecting their health needs to be provided.

Unequal Counterparts

The President has proposed health care *choice* for all Americans. It is inappropriate and contrary to the principles of the President's plan for military families to be the only ones singled out for limited choice, quality, and access to physicians. Not only do active and retired military families under 65 not have any funded entitlement to health care, they have no health insurance at all—since TRICARE is not an insurance program. Federal employees and federal retirees of all ages, on the other hand, are entitled to FEHBP, which provides over 200 choices of health insurance.

Further, the VA/TRICARE—But Not Both! policy of the Administration would also make military retirees still more uniquely disadvantaged. They would become the only federal retirees not to keep the health care coverage they earned during a lifetime of service. Federal civilian employees would keep their FEHBP *and* still have access to the VA [Veterans Administration] if they were veterans; military retirees would have to choose, even though the two systems were designed for entirely different purposes.

Many military retirees use VA because TRICARE is not accepted by civilian doctors in the areas where they live. Still other military retirees use DVA [Department of Veterans Affairs] because of disabilities incurred during their military careers. TRICARE, in fact, refers military retirees to the DVA for disability related services that TRICARE does not provide. As an example, hearing aids and other prosthetic devices can be prescribed to DVA patients based on service connected disabilities and other criteria, but TRICARE does not offer these services to military retirees.

TRICARE is a very complex and contradictory for-profit experiment that has broken promises and dashed expectations of the nation's professional volunteer soldiers and their families. It has impinged upon the honor, dignity and respect military families who were promised more for their noble service. . . .

Key Complaints

Active and retired military families earn(ed) and expect(ed) excellent, low or no-cost health care as part of their basic compensation, in return for reduced salaries that were expressly reduced based on specific high cash values for that care. Instead, they received neither the cash their federal civilian counterparts are paid to buy health insurance, nor the funded legal entitlement their federal civilian counterparts have for health care. Neither do they have the excellent, affordable range of choices of health care programs their federal civilian counterparts have.

Military families have only an "in-kind" benefit—a one-of-a-kind federal program that leaves little choice to meet family needs and budgets, and fails in some cases to provide even the most rudimentary access to medical care.

In the case of TRICARE Standard, the only real choice is to use it or not. Even that choice is often taken away from them by physicians who refuse to see them under the TRI-CARE program, or through the onerous requirement to change physicians in mid-stream in serious medical situations because of the DOD-unique non-availability statement system.

Instead of valuing the user, as the key link in the system, the TRICARE system appears to place the major burden on the *users*—the beneficiaries, and the least burden on the contractors and employees who operate the system for profit. There is extreme frustration in many cases with trying to obtain customer satisfaction when frequent problems occur.

This is an insult to many of those who served the longest. While some users are satisfied with the part of TRICARE that applies to them, a large number are not. Those most dissatisfied are families on TRICARE Standard, which is about half the eligible population of 8.8 million, largely retiree families, since about 85 percent of the active duty force use TRICARE Prime. Many families consider the problems [related to TRI-CARE] as intolerable. The problems are likely to affect all potential users at some point, and have left some families, who served lifetime careers, without medical coverage at all or with worse treatment than that afforded our nation's enemies and prisoners in federal prisons.

Reading Between the Lines

It is especially frustrating to see official glossy publications produced jointly by government and contract civilian TRI-CARE program operators (the true beneficiaries) declaring that the problems with TRICARE have been largely solved, when the opposite is true. It is also telling that the annual TRICARE Management Activity official 2000 and 2001 "STAKEHOLDER reports concerning TRICARE" totally exclude mention of TRICARE Standard and its problems, while focusing on TRICARE Prime, which is either not available, or appropriate for, approximately half the eligible DOD population.

We believe that Congress and DOD do not recognize the depth of the problems . . . and certainly do not understand that they have NOT been solved. We commend these systemic problems to the congressional and DOD leadership, in hopes that improvements will be initiated immediately to respond to the users who *earned* decent care.

4

The Veterans TRICARE System of Health Care Improves Each Year

S. Ward Casscells

S. Ward Casscells, a physician, became U.S. assistant secretary of defense for health affairs in 2007, with oversight responsibility for the health and medical affairs of the Department of Defense. Also a colonel in the U.S. Army Reserve, he is the author of numerous articles on a wide range of health policy issues.

Americans, both military and civilian, have high expectations for the medical care and benefits available to veterans. The military TRICARE system has met and exceeded those expectations. Overall satisfaction with the TRICARE program continues to grow, as benefits expand in both scope and substance to reach more veterans and their families. But such expansion costs money. Military engagements in the Middle East as well as worldwide humanitarian missions have created palpable strain on the veterans' health care system, despite its successes. If Americans are truly committed to providing the very best medical care for veterans, they must support a Congress that is willing to wisely allocate and spend precious taxpayer dollars.

The MHS [Military Health System] serves more than 2.2 million members of the Active, Reserve, and Guard components with more than 251,000 service members deployed overseas.

S. Ward Casscells, "The Military Health System," testimony Before the U.S. Congressional Committee on Appropriations, Subcommittee on Defense, May 2, 2007. Available at http://www.dod.mil/dodgc/olc/docs/testCasscells070502.pdf.

The Department [of Defense, or DoD] is committed to protecting the health of our service members and to providing the best healthcare to more than 9 million eligible beneficiaries. . . .

Our primary objective is ensuring that every service member is medically protected and fit for duty. Together with the military commanders, we use a variety of tools to achieve this outcome.

Based on outcomes data, process measures, and independent assessments by healthcare organizations around the country, our military medical personnel have performed extraordinarily on the battlefield and in our medical facilities in the United States. We are proud of these accomplishments—improving virtually every major category of wartime medicine, and many areas of peacetime medicine:

- Lowest Disease, Non Battle Injury (DNBI) Rate. As a testament to training, medical readiness and preparedness, preventive medicine approach and occupational health capabilities, we are successfully addressing the single largest contributor to loss of forces—disease. The present DNBI rates for Operation Enduring Freedom (OEF) [the war in Afghanistan begun in 2002] and Operation Iraqi Freedom (OIF) [the war on Iraq begun 2003] are the lowest ever reported, 5% and 4% respectively. By comparison, the DNBI rates in Desert Shield/ Desert Storm [Kuwait] were 6.5% per week, Operation Joint Endeavor (Bosnia) were 7.1% per week, and Operation Joint Guardian (Kosovo) were 8.1% per week.

- Lowest Death to Wounded Ratio. Our agility in reaching wounded service members, and capability in treating them, has altered our perspective on what constitutes timeliness in life-saving care from the "golden hour" to the "platinum fifteen minutes." We are saving lives of wounded troops who would not have survived even 10 years ago. For example, almost 88% of those wounded in Afghanistan and Iraq survive, compared with 75% in World War II and 81% in Vietnam.

- Reduced time to evacuation. We now expedite the evacuation of service members following forward-deployed surgery to stateside definitive care. Using airborne intensive care units and the latest technology, we have been able to move wounded service members from the battlefield to the highest quality of definitive care in the United States in as little as 48 hours.

- Our medical professionals provide high-quality medical care, and our quality indicators compare very favorably with national benchmarks. The DoD Patient Safety Program is a national model. TeamSTEPPS, which is a part of our Patient Safety Program, is a national model for improving communication and teamwork skills. We have achieved significant results through our efforts to reduce medical errors. . . .

At the direction of Congress, we executed new health benefits which extend TRICARE coverage to members of the National Guard and Reserve.

At the direction of Congress, we executed new health benefits which extend TRICARE coverage to members of the National Guard and Reserve. We implemented the TRICARE Reserve Select (TRS) health plan for Reserve Component personnel and their families. We are now working on the expanded program mandated by the NDAA [National Defense Authorization Act] for FY [fiscal year] 2007. Today, more than 34,000 reservists and their families are paying premiums to receive TRS coverage. In addition, we made permanent their early access to TRICARE upon receipt of call-up orders and their continued access to TRICARE for six months following active duty service for both individuals and their families. Our FY 2008 budget request includes $381 million to cover the costs of this expanded benefit. . . .

Our primary mission is sustaining a medically ready military force and providing world-class health services for those injured and wounded in combat.

The Cost of Good Care

Our primary mission is sustaining a medically ready military force and providing world-class health services for those injured and wounded in combat. Yet, our resources are not unlimited. . . .

Despite efficiently managing healthcare costs and utilizing a variety of initiatives, we have much work to do. We continue to use a number of proven means to reduce healthcare costs in our system. These include:

- Obtaining significant savings for pharmaceuticals at our MTFs [military treatment facilities] and mail-order venue when compared to the retail point of service. The acquisition price of brand-name drugs, which represent the bulk of pharmaceutical expenditures in DoD, average 25 percent to 40 percent less at MTFs and mail-order when compared to retail.

- Implementing the new TRICARE pharmacy Uniform formulary. We estimate savings of more than $500 million in just the past two years due to key formulary-management changes and decisions.

- Contract strategies. Effective TRICARE contracting strategies have reduced administrative costs, and our effort to further enhance the next generation of the TRICARE contract is well underway. Once again, our

Chief Financial Officer estimates several hundreds of millions of dollars in savings due to these new contracts.

- Further increases in VA [Veterans Administration] and DoD sharing of facilities, capabilities, and joint procurements.

- The introduction of new prime vendor agreements to lower costs of MTF medical and surgical supplies. The MHS has aggressively negotiated preferential pricings with medical-supply vendors across the country, and we project cost avoidance of $28.3 million. . . .

Congressional Support Is Imperative

As you know, the Department is challenged by the growing costs of the MHS. We need important changes in our well-regarded health benefit program, TRICARE, to sustain a superior benefit for the long term. We need the help and support of Congress to achieve this goal. Our FY 2008 budget request assumes savings of $2.2 billion from reform proposals (as projected last year for FY 2008); we await the interim report of the Department of Defense Task Force on the Future of Military Health Care as a basis for dialogue with the Congress on how these should be shaped.

The benefit enhancements have come at a time when private-sector employers are shifting substantially more costs to employees for their healthcare.

As the civil and military leaders of the Department have testified, we must place the health benefit program on a sound fiscal foundation or face adverse consequences. Costs have more than doubled in six years—from $19 billion in FY 2001 to $39 billion in FY 2007—despite MHS management actions to make the system more efficient. Our analysts project this program will cost taxpayers at least $64 billion by 2015. Healthcare costs will continue to consume a growing slice of the Department's budget, reaching 12 percent of the budget by 2015 (versus 4.5 percent in 1990).

Over the last 13 years, the TRICARE benefit was enhanced through reductions in co-pays, expansions in covered services (particularly for Medicare-eligible beneficiaries), new benefits for the Reserve Component, and other additions, but the premiums paid by beneficiaries have not changed. The benefit enhancements have come at a time when private-sector employers are shifting substantially more costs to employees for their healthcare.

The twin effect of greater benefits for DOD beneficiaries at no change in premiums, coupled with reduced benefits for military retirees employed in second careers in the private sector, has led to a significant increase in military retirees electing to drop their private health insurance and become entirely reliant on TRICARE for their health benefit. Some employers actively encourage this shift through incentives to their employees.

Simply put, the Department and Congress must work together to allow the Department to make necessary changes to the TRICARE benefit to better manage the long-term cost structure of our program. Failure to do so will harm military healthcare and the overall capabilities of the Department of Defense—outcomes we cannot afford.

5

Veterans Returning from Combat Are Not Getting Proper Medical Care

Bobby Muller

Bobby Muller is a longtime activist working for the rights of veterans; he is the president of Veterans for America (VFA). In 1980 he founded the Vietnam Veterans for America Foundation, which later became the VFA, an advocacy and humanitarian organization focusing primarily on the needs of veterans and active service members who have served in the wars in Afghanistan and Iraq.

When fellow citizens risk their lives to serve their country in the military, the U.S. government and citizenry have a moral obligation to ensure that such service and the sacrifice it often entails was not for naught. To that end, the government must provide veterans with the best equipment and training while they are deployed and take care of their service-related needs when they return. Vietnam veterans were not given adequate care upon their return, and the same is true of service members today. The programs and services offered through the Veterans Administration (VA) do not meet the needs of today's veterans and their families. The American public should pull together and pressure the government to take better care of service members.

A s we enter the fifth year [in May 2007] of our nation's war in Iraq, I am deeply distressed by the state of the American military and by the rate at which our government and the citizenry at large are betraying those who volunteer to serve our country. There is a social contract between a country and those it sends to fight for it, and America's social contract is broken. When citizens are willing to serve, risking their lives for America, our government has a corresponding moral obligation to ensure—before, during and after deployment—that such willingness is not squandered. First, the government ought to ensure that deployment is absolutely necessary. The conflict must be worthy of the sacrifices being asked. Decisions that require the greatest sacrifice from the citizens must be subjected to full congressional and public debate. Second, when our nation deploys troops, the government must provide the capacity, the strategy, the numbers, the equipment and any other support our troops require. Today it is clear that our service members are not getting the support they deserve. Third, when service members pay a personal price in serving our country, the government must ensure that when they return, health, rehabilitative and readjustment programs can provide adequately for their specific needs. Everyone in America should realize that these criteria are not being met today.

We must begin to distribute the sacrifice equitably, not by sharing the burden of combat but through active political engagement.

The Most Important of All

The third part of the social contract deserves greater attention and elaboration. The system currently in place to deal with the needs of returning service members and veterans needs repair. Thirty-eight years ago, while I was serving in Vietnam, an enemy bullet ripped through my chest as I led an assault against a hill, just below the demilitarized zone, defended by North Vietnamese regular forces. It is a miracle that I survived, albeit as a paraplegic confined to a wheelchair. The military medical evacuation was the best in the world. I was flown out to the hospital ship, the U.S.S. *Repose*, and given immediate life-saving surgery. The care was spectacular.

When I entered long-term rehabilitation, however, things went downhill fast. My first day in the New York City veterans' hospital, where I was to stay as a patient for a year, was the first time I cried since being wounded. I was overwhelmed with despair at the circumstances in which I found myself. *Life* magazine depicted my ward as a "medical slum." When my government asked me to serve, I did. I paid an immense personal price, and my country subsequently turned its back on me. I had been betrayed. As the war began to wind down and the people became aware that the government had lied about the necessity and purposefulness of the war, I became very angry. The betrayal I felt was debilitating.

For more than 35 years now, I have fought for service member and veterans benefits. I used to believe that the changes enacted as a result of our struggles would lead to better care for future generations. It was my hope that no service member or veteran would ever again feel a similar sense of betrayal by our country. But I was wrong.

Today's service members and veterans are being forced to fight the same battles we fought. It is shameful. How is it possible that America has not learned from its mistakes? How is it possible that as a nation we collectively ignore the challenges of service members until the suffering and neglect become horrifying?

New Challenges

The 1.5 million service members and veterans who have served our country in the ongoing wars in Iraq and Afghanistan are desperate for programs that address their specific needs. It is important to understand that each new war brings with it a new set of challenges for returning service members. It is also important to realize that the demographics of today's military differ dramatically from those of any previous military force this country has sent to war. The American Psychological Association recently released a report, titled *The Psychological Needs of U.S. Military Service Members and Their Families*, which found that no one has done the basic research to understand the unique needs of today's military.

The appalling conditions revealed at Walter Reed [Army Medical Center in Washington, D.C.] were not simply the consequence of poor maintenance or budgetary neglect. Rather, the conditions represent a basic failure by the Department of Defense and the Veterans Administration to respond to the new set of challenges faced by those who have returned from duty in Iraq and Afghanistan.

It was not until 10 years after the height of the war in Vietnam that post-traumatic stress disorder [P.T.S.D.] was recognized as a medical condition and that Vet Centers were created to help Vietnam veterans cope with the mental health and other readjustment challenges created by their military service. It took 15 years to complete a study of the Vietnam generation. During that time, thousands upon thousands of lives were ruined by a system that failed to recognize and respond to urgent service-connected challenges. It ought not happen again. Yet by many indications, it appears to be recurring. If such recovery programs are not in place, it matters little whether the Department of Defense and the VA have the best doctors, equipment, recordkeeping and medicine money can buy.

Soldiers Are Now Older and Include Women

Today's soldiers are older than those who served in Vietnam. Since Sept. 11, 2001, the average age of those deployed for combat is 27, as compared with 19 for combat soldiers in Vietnam, virtually all of whom were single men. Iraq/ Afghanistan, by contrast, is a family war; 60 percent of those deployed have family responsibilities, and 47 percent of those who have died have left families behind. Those deployed to Iraq and Afghanistan include 160,000 women, 16,000 of whom (1 in 10) are single mothers.

According to *The New York Times*, "A 2003 report financed by the Department of Defense revealed that nearly one-third of a nationwide sample of female veterans seeking health care through the VA said they experienced rape or attempted rape during their service. Of that group, 37 percent said they were raped multiple times, and 14 percent reported they were gang-raped." Despite these statistics, the VA currently has only two in-patient programs for women with service-connected P.T.S.D.

The average age of members of the Guard and Reserve is even higher, at 33. The Department of Defense and the Veterans Administration are not meeting their recruitment goals. They must rectify a striking disparity: members of the National Guard and the Reserve are half as likely to file a VA claim as members of the active component, and Guard and Reserve members are twice as likely to have their claims rejected. This is unacceptable. Such staggering examples of neglect reveal a system that is inadequate to the needs of our newest generation of warriors.

Stepping Up to the Plate

It is important to understand that our broken social contract is symptomatic of a country disengaged from its own wars. Fewer than half of 1 percent of our population is shouldering the burden (and taking on the life-and-death risk) of this "long war." With an all-volunteer military, most of the country can remain oblivious to its horrors. This must change. We must begin to distribute the sacrifice equitably, not by sharing the burden of combat but through active political engagement. The American public can create a strong social contract. We can pressure our government to uphold its end of the bargain, knowing that our service members need our action. Collectively we can reverse the betrayal felt by this generation. Whether we like it or not, these are our wars, and we must begin to take ownership of their causes, conduct and consequences. What does America—its government and its citizens—owe to those who serve? We owe them a social contract worthy of their sacrifice.

6

Wounded Veterans Returning from Combat Receive Excellent Medical Care

George W. Bush

George W. Bush is the forty-third president of the United States (2001–2009).

Americans would truly be impressed with the caregivers who tend to the needs of our returning veterans at hospitals like Walter Reed Army Medical Center. The problems that have plagued the veterans' health care system are not ones of medical care. Rather, they involve bureaucratic and administrative failures. The U.S. government has taken many steps to improve this system. The secretary of defense has demanded accountability and made changes in leadership, including the appointment of a nonmedical deputy commander. A new task force of cabinet officers will identify potential gaps in services, and a bipartisan presidential commission will conduct a comprehensive overview of the care available to veterans. The military system is large and complex, but regardless of the obstacles, the nation owes wounded service members the best care available.

Every time I come to Walter Reed, my spirits are lifted. They're first lifted by the soldiers and marines who are recovering from some very tough wounds. I had the honor of pinning the Purple Heart on quite a few people, and I am always impressed by their resolve and their commitment to the

George W. Bush, "Remarks During a Visit to Walter Reed Army Medical Center," *Weekly Compilation of Presidential Documents*, vol. 33, April 2, 2007, pp. 389–391.

country. Every time I come to Walter Reed, I'm also impressed by the caregivers—the docs, the nurses, the people who spend many hours trying to heal those who have been wounded in service to our country.

The soldiers and marines stay here only for a few months, but the compassion they receive here stays with them for a lifetime.

The soldiers and marines stay here only for a few months, but the compassion they receive here stays with them for a lifetime. And so on behalf of a grateful nation, I do want to thank our docs and our nurses and caregivers for providing extraordinary health care to the people who wear the uniform. I know full well that the work you do is behind the scenes. In other words, you don't get a lot of glory for what you do, but you certainly do from the family members who first come here, and they see their loved one on a bed, wondering whether or not that person will ever walk again. And then, 6 months later, the body is returning, and the spirit is strong—the person is up and moving around: The family and the soldier is impressed by that care.

Care Is Excellent

Americans must understand that the problems recently uncovered at Walter Reed were not the problems of medical care. The quality of care at this fantastic facility is great, and it needs to remain that way. Independent analyses have given extremely high marks for the quality of care here. In other words, this isn't my assessment, nor is it the assessment of people I have talked to—the families, although that's what they believe. It is also the assessment of a joint commission, which accredits thousands of American hospitals. And this commission has given Walter Reed the highest possible rating, a gold seal of approval.

Recently, the commission performed a surprise inspection. In other words, they didn't give a bunch of notice; they showed up and verified the high quality of care here. I want to congratulate you for what you're doing.

The system failed you, and it failed our troops.

System Failure

The problems at Walter Reed were caused by bureaucratic and administrative failures. The system failed you, and it failed our troops. And we're going to fix it.

I met some of the soldiers who had been housed in Building 18 [allegedly the most rundown of the one hundred buildings there]. I was disturbed by their accounts of what went wrong. It is not right to have someone volunteer to wear our uniform and not get the best possible care. I apologize for what they went through, and we're going to fix the problem.

And that's exactly what this Government is going to do. We're not going to be satisfied until everybody gets the kind of care that their folks and families expect. And that's what I expect. And we've taken important steps to achieve the objective.

Palpable Changes

First, Defense Secretary [Robert M.] Gates has insisted on accountability in the military command. He made changes in leadership. He made tough decisions, because he, like me, demands results. I welcome General [Peter J.] Schoomaker, but I also welcome General [Michael S.] Tucker. Tucker is not a doc. As General Schoomaker informed me, he is a "bureaucracy buster." His job is to make sure that the bureaucracy does not get in the way of making sure every soldier, marine, and their families get the best possible care. And I welcome you to the command, and thank you.

Secretary Gates, as I said, has approved a non-medical deputy commander—that's Tucker. Building 18 has been closed. We're fixing that which needs to be fixed, including, interestingly enough, putting a new roof on it. The patients from Building 18 have been transferred into Abrams Hall, and I'm pleased to report that living conditions there are of high quality.

We have formed three working groups to help address problems that may exist and may arise. I want to share some of what the strategy behind the working groups is, and that is, first, Secretary Gates established an independent review group, and that was primarily to examine the conditions at Walter Reed and Bethesda [Naval Hospital]. The group will recommend ways to ensure you have what you need to improve medical care.

Being a Good Listener

I heard one recommendation, in other words, one of the care providers said, "Make sure we always have the best possible equipment; we want to be on the leading edge of technology, not the trailing edge." I agree completely. Those are the kinds of things that Secretary Gates's commission is going to be looking into.

[Then-]Veterans Affairs Secretary [R. James] Nicholson is leading a task force of Cabinet officers to identify potential gaps in the services our wounded troops receive as they return from the battlefield. In other words, we want all hands on deck here at the Federal level to make sure that health care is as good as it possibly can be. I'm not talking about the health care in the operating room; I'm talking about the bureaucracies that may prevent good health care from being delivered.

Finally, [then-senator] Bob Dole and [then-secretary of health and human services] Donna Shalala will chair a bipartisan Presidential Commission on care for our wounded warriors. They will conduct a comprehensive view of the entire

51

system for providing physical and emotional care to service men and women injured in [the Iraq] war. They will make sure that that person gets high-quality care from the time they suffer their wounds through their return to civilian life.

We want to make sure, for example, that any transfer from the Defense Department to the Veterans Affairs Department is smooth and that there's not bureaucratic delay or obstacles in the way of making sure that we can report to our fellow citizens that people are getting the best possible health care.

I want to thank those who are working in these groups, and I'm looking forward to getting their recommendations, because I want to make sure our military families can be assured that their loved ones will get the very best.

None of the problems that we have uncovered can overshadow the great work you do.

And so our Nation is grateful, and I'm proud to be your Commander in Chief.

The Best Care Possible

This military system of ours, when you really think about it, just across the country, it's very complex, and it's large. Yet there's nothing complex about what we owe our troops; we owe them the best. That's what you believe here at Walter Reed. I have seen the care and dedication that you give on a daily basis. I just came from the therapy rooms, the physical therapy and the vocational therapy rooms. I see people patiently working with a wounded soldier on how to pick up cards and play cards with a new prosthesis. It's just hours of help all because the people here recognize each human being matters, each person counts, and each person has endless possibilities, even though they may have received terrible wounds on the battlefield.

None of the problems that we have uncovered can overshadow the great work you do here. That's what you have to know. It's a special calling to serve those who serve our country. It requires a unique person to come here on a daily basis and to heal the hurts of those who served our country.

7

The VA Is Not Prepared to Meet the Long-Term Care Needs of Returning Vets

Linda Bilmes

Linda Bilmes is a lecturer in public policy, as well as a professor of budgeting and public finance at the Kennedy School of Government, Harvard University. She served as assistant secretary for management and budget in the U.S. Department of Commerce during the administration of President Bill Clinton. In addition to numerous research papers and articles, she has written a book, The People Factor, *about civil service reform.*

Advances in equipment and in medical care have meant that more wounded soldiers survive their injuries, a fact that has contributed to a significant rise in the need for health care for veterans. The U.S. government must be prepared to meet veterans' immediate as well as long-term needs by increasing funds and improving the structure of the Department of Veterans Affairs. Two of the most significant long-term costs of war are veterans' disability benefits and their medical care. Studies indicate three major obstacles facing the government: The already overwhelmed Veterans Health Administration will not be able to provide high-quality care in a timely fashion to the massive wave of returning veterans without greater funding and increased capacity. In addition, the Veterans Benefits Administration is already burdened with the current volume of claims and will be unable to cope with the high volume of pending claims. Finally, the budgetary costs of providing medical and disability care and benefits to veterans over the course of their lifetimes will be staggering.

The New Year [January 2007] has brought with it the grim fact that 3000 American soldiers have been killed so far in Iraq. A statistic that merits equal attention is the unprecedented number of US soldiers who have been injured. As of September 30, 2006, more than 50,500 US soldiers have suffered non-mortal wounds in Iraq, Afghanistan and nearby staging locations—a ratio of 16 wounded servicemen for every fatality. This is by far the highest killed-to-wounded ratio in US history. For example, in the Vietnam and Korean wars there were 2.6 and 2.8 injuries per fatality, respectively. World Wars I and II had fewer than 2 wounded servicemen per death.

All 1.4 million servicemen deployed in the [Iraq] war effort are potentially eligible to claim some level of disability compensation from the Veterans Benefits Administration.

While it is welcome news and a credit to military medicine that more soldiers are surviving grievous wounds, the existence of so many veterans, with such a high level of injuries, is yet another aspect of this war for which the Pentagon and the Administration failed to plan, prepare and budget. There are significant costs and requirements in caring for our wounded veterans, including medical treatment and long-term health care, the payment of disability compensation, pensions and other benefits, reintegration assistance and counseling, and providing the statistical documentation necessary to move veterans seamlessly from the Department of Defense payroll into Department of Veterans Affairs medical care, and to process VA [Veterans Administration] disability claims easily.

Assessing the Magnitude

To date, 1.4 million US servicemen have been deployed to the Global War on Terror (GWOT), the Pentagon's name for operations in and around Iraq and Afghanistan. The servicemen who have been officially wounded are a small percentage of the veterans who will be using the veteran's administration medical system. Hundreds of thousands of these men and women will be seeking medical care and claiming disability compensation for a wide variety of disabilities that they incurred during their tours of duty. The cost of providing such care and paying disability compensation is a significant long-term entitlement cost that the US will be paying for the next forty years. . . .

All 1.4 million servicemen deployed in the current war effort are potentially eligible to claim some level of disability compensation from the Veterans Benefits Administration. Disability compensation is a monetary benefit paid to veterans with "service-connected disabilities"—meaning that the disability was the result of an illness, disease or injury incurred or aggravated while the soldier was on active military service. Veterans are not required to seek employment nor are there any other conditions attached to the program. The explicit congressional intent in providing this benefit is "to compensate for a reduction in quality of life due to service-connected disability" and to "provide compensation for average impairment in earnings capacity." The principle dates back to the Bible at Exodus 21:25, which authorizes financial compensation for pain inflicted by another.

Disability compensation is graduated according to the degree of the veteran's disability, on a scale from 0 percent to 100 percent, in increments of 10 percent. Annual benefits range from a low of $1304 per year for a veteran with a 10 percent disability rating to about $44,000 in annual benefits for those who are completely disabled. The average benefit is $8890, although this varies considerably; Vietnam veterans average about $11,670. Additional benefits and pensions are payable to veterans with severe disabilities. Once deemed eligible, the veteran receives the compensation payment as a mandatory entitlement for the remainder of their lives, like Medicare and Social Security.

Where the Line Is Drawn

There is no statute of limitations on the amount of time a veteran can claim for most disability benefits. The majority of veteran's claims are within the first few years after returning, but some disabilities do not surface until years later. The VA is still handling hundreds of thousands of new claims from Vietnam era veterans for post-traumatic stress disorder [PTSD] and cancers linked to Agent Orange exposure.

Most employees at VA are themselves veterans, and are predisposed to assisting veterans obtain the maximum amount of benefits to which they are entitled.

The process for ascertaining whether a veteran is suffering from a disability, and determining the percentage level of a veteran's disability, is complicated and lengthy. A veteran must apply to one of the 57 regional offices of the Veterans Benefits Administration (VBA), where a claims adjudicator evaluates the veteran's service-connected impairments and assigns a rating for the degree to which the veteran is disabled. For veterans with multiple disabilities, the regional office combines the ratings into a single composite rating. If a veteran disagrees with the regional office's decision he or she can file an appeal to the VA's Board of Veterans Appeals. The Board makes a final decision and can grant or deny benefits or send the case back to the regional office for further evaluation. Typically a veteran applies for disability in more than one category, for example, a mental health condition as well as a skin disorder. In such cases, VBA can decide to approve only part of the

claim—which often results in the veteran appealing the decision. If the veteran is still dissatisfied with the Board's decision to grant service connection or the percentage rating, he
or she can further appeal it to two even higher levels of
decision-makers.

Most employees at VA are themselves veterans, and are
predisposed to assisting veterans obtain the maximum amount
of benefits to which they are entitled. However, the process itself is long, cumbersome, inefficient and paperwork-intensive.
The process for approving claims has been the subject of numerous GAO [Government Accountability Office] studies and
investigations over the years. Even in 2000, before the [Iraq]
war, GAO identified longstanding problems in the claims processing area. These included large backlogs of pending claims,
lengthy processing times for initial claims, high error rates in
claims processing, and inconsistency across regional offices. In
a 2005 study, GAO found that the time to complete a veteran's
claim varied from 99 days at the Salt Lake City regional office
to 237 days at the Honolulu, Hawaii office.

The backlog of pending claims has been growing since
1996. In 2000, VBA had a backlog of 69,000 pending initial
compensation claims, of which one-third had been pending
for more than six months. Today [2007] due in part to the
surge in claims from the Iraq/Afghan wars, VBA has a backlog
of 400,000 claims. VBA now takes an average of 177 days (six
months) to process an original claim, and an average of 657
days (nearly two years) to process an appeal. This compares
unfavorably with the private sector health care/financial services industry, which processes an annual 30 billion claims in
an average of 89.5 days per claim, *including* the time required
for claims that are disputed.

Calculating the Incalculable

It is difficult to predict with certainty the number of veterans
from the [Iraq/Afghan] wars who will claim for some amount

of disability. The first Gulf War provides a baseline number although the Iraq and Afghanistan war has been longer and has involved more ground warfare than the Desert Storm conflict, which relied largely on aerial bombardment and four days of intense ground combat. However, in both conflicts, a number of veterans were exposed to depleted uranium that was used in anti-tank rounds fired by US M1 tanks and US A10 attack aircraft. Many disability claims from the first Gulf War stem from exposure to depleted uranium, which has been implicated in raising the risk of cancers and birth defects. Gulf War veterans also filed disability claims related to exposures to oil well fire pollution, low-levels of chemical warfare agents, experimental anthrax vaccines, and experimental anti-chemical warfare agent pills called pyridostigmine bromide, the anti-malaria pill Lariam, skin diseases, and disorders from living in the hot climate, which are likely to be cited in the [Iraq/Afghan] conflict. However, the number of disability claims in the Iraq/Afghan wars is likely to be higher due to the significantly longer length of soldier's deployments, repeat deployments, and heavier exposure to urban combat.

Following the Gulf War the criteria for receiving benefits were widened by Congress based on evidence of widespread toxic exposures. The same criteria for healthcare and benefits eligibility still apply to veterans of the Iraq and Afghanistan wars. Forty-four percent of those veterans filed disability claims for a variety of conditions and 87 percent were approved. The US currently pays about $4 billion annually in disability payments to veterans of Desert Storm/Desert Shield.

Of the 1.4 million US servicemen who have so far been deployed in the Iraq/Afghan conflicts, 631,174 have been discharged as of September 30, 2006. Of those, 46 percent are in the full-time military and 54 percent are reservists and National Guardsmen. Therefore the total population that is potentially eligible for disability benefits is this number (631,174). To date 152,669 servicemen have applied for disability benefits and of those, 104,819 have been granted, 34,405 are pending and 13,445 have been rejected. This implies an approval rate of 88 percent to date. . . .

System Overload

The issue is not simply cost but also efficiency in providing disabled veterans with their benefits. In addition to all the problems detailed above, the Iraq and Afghan war veterans are filing claims of unusually high complexity. To date, the backlog of pending claims from these recent war veterans is 34,000, but the vast majority of servicemen from this conflict have not yet filed their claims. Even without the projected wave of claims, the VA has an overall backlog of 400,000, including thousands of Vietnam era claims. Including all pending claims and other paperwork, the VA's backlog has increased from 465,623 in 2004 to 525,270 in 2005 to 604,380 in 2006.

The VA's Veterans Health Administration provides medical care to more than 5 million veterans each year.

The fact that the VBA is largely sympathetic to the plight of disabled veterans should not obscure the fact that this system is already under tremendous strain. . . .

The VA's Veterans Health Administration provides medical care to more than 5 million veterans each year. This care includes primary and secondary care, as well as dental, eye and mental health care, hospital inpatient and outpatient services. The care is free to all returning veterans for the first two years after they return from active duty; thereafter the VA imposes co-payments for various services, with the amounts related to the level of disability of the veteran.

Sacrificing Quality for Volume

The VA has long prided itself on the excellence of care that it provides to veterans. In particular, VA hospitals and clinics are known to perform a heroic job in areas such as rehabilitation.

Medical staff is experienced in working with veterans and provides a sympathetic and supportive environment for those who are disabled. It is therefore of utmost importance that the quality of care be maintained as the demand for it goes up.

However, the demand for VA medical treatment is far exceeding what the VA had anticipated. This has produced long waiting lists and in some cases simply the absence of care. To date, 205,097, or 32 percent of the 631,174 eligible discharged OEF [Operation Enduring Freedom, the war in Afghanistan begun in 2002]/OIF [Operation Iraqi Freedom, the war in Iraq begun in 2003] veterans have sought treatment at VA health facilities. These include 35 percent of the eligible active duty servicemen (101,260) and 31 percent of the eligible Reservists/Guards (103,837). To date, this number represents only 4 percent of the total patient visits at VA facilities—but it will grow. According to the VA, "As in other cohorts of military veterans, the percentage of OIF/OEF veterans receiving medical care from the VA and the percentage of veterans with any type of diagnosis will tend to increase over time as these veterans continue to enroll for VA health care and to develop new health problems."

The war in Iraq has been noteworthy for the types of injuries sustained by the soldiers. Some 20 percent have suffered brain trauma, spinal injuries or amputations; another 20 percent have suffered other major injuries such as amputations, blindness, partial blindness or deafness, and serious burns.

However, the largest unmet need is in the area of mental health care. The strain of extended deployments, the stop-loss policy, stressful ground warfare and uncertainty regarding discharge and leave has taken an especially high toll on soldiers. Thirty-six percent of the veterans treated so far—an unprecedented number—have been diagnosed with a mental health condition. These include PTSD, acute depression, substance abuse and other conditions. According to Paul Sullivan, a leading veterans advocate, "The signature wounds from the wars will be (1) traumatic brain injury, (2) post-traumatic stress disorder, (3) amputations and (4) spinal cord injuries, and PTSD will be the most controversial and most expensive.". . .

Vet Centers Offer Some Solutions

How can the VA possibly handle the number of returning troops who require care, as well as their families, especially for mental health conditions? Perhaps the most creative and successful innovation in the VA in the past two decades has been the introduction of the "Vet Centers"—207 walk-in storefront centers where veterans or their families can obtain counseling and reintegration assistance. The centers, operated by VA's "Readjustment Counseling Service" are popular with veterans and their families and—at a total cost of some $100 million per year—provide a highly cost-effective option for veterans who are not in need of acute medical care. The Vet Centers are particularly helpful for families; for example, they provide a venue for a soldier's spouse to seek guidance if the veteran is showing mental distress but will not seek help. They also supply bereavement counseling to surviving families of those killed during military service. And they offer a friendlier environment, often staffed with recent OEF/OIF combat veterans and other war veterans—unlike VA regional offices which tend to be stuffy, bureaucratic offices located in downtown locations. . . .

> *Overall, the US is not adequately prepared for the influx of returning servicemen from Iraq and Afghanistan.*

Facing the Future

Overall the US is not adequately prepared for the influx of returning servicemen from Iraq and Afghanistan. There are three major areas in which it is not prepared: claims processing capacity for disability benefits; medical treatment capacity, in terms of the number of health care personnel available at clinics throughout the country, particularly in mental health; and third, there is no preparation for paying the cost of another major entitlement program.

As discussed earlier, the backlog in claims benefits is already somewhere between 400,000 and 600,000. Unless major changes are made to this process, the number of claims pending and requiring attention will reach some 750,000 within the next two years and the pendency period will increase proportionately, resulting in more veterans falling though the cracks that could have been avoided. In addition, veterans whose claims reach different centers in different parts of the country will have widely different experiences, proving highly unfair to those who just happen to be located in areas of greater backlog.

The quality of medical care is likely to continue to be high for veterans with serious injuries treated in VA's new polytrauma centers. However, the current supply of care makes it unlikely that all facilities can offer veterans a high quality of care in a timely fashion. Veterans with mental health conditions are most likely to be at risk because of the lack of manpower and the inability of those scheduling appointments to distinguish between higher and lower risk conditions. If the current trends continue, the VA is likely to see demand for health care rising to 750,000 veterans in the next few years, which will overwhelm the system in terms of scheduling, diagnostic testing, and visiting specialists, especially in some regions.

The cost of providing disability benefits and medical care, even under the most optimistic scenario that no additional troops are deployed and the claims pattern is only that of the previous Gulf War, would suggest that at a minimum the cost of providing lifetime disability benefits and medical care is $350 billion. If the number of unique troops increases by another 200,000 to 500,000 over a period of years, this number may rise to as high as nearly $700 billion. The funding needs for veterans' benefits thus comprise an additional major entitlement program along with MediCare and Social Security that will need to be financed through borrowing if the US remains in deficit. This will in turn place further pressure on all discretionary spending including that for additional veterans' medical care.

Veteran's disability benefits and medical care are two of the most significant long-term costs of the war. . . .

Effecting Palpable Change

The Veterans Health Administration will not be able to sustain its high quality of care without greater funding and increased capacity in areas such as psychiatric care and brain trauma units. In addition, more funding should be provided for readjustment counseling services by social workers at the Vet Centers. Even doubling the amount of funding for counseling at the Vet Centers is a small amount compared to the funds now being requested for additional recruiting of new soldiers.

There are at least three potential methods of reducing the number of pending claims. Perhaps the easiest would be to "fast track" returning Iraq and Afghan war veteran's claims in a single center staffed with highly experienced group of adjudicators who could provide most veterans with a decision within 90 days. At a minimum, all simple claims could be dispatched in this manner. During the past decade, private sector health insurance companies have reengineered their processes and adopted technologies, such as new automated data capture and document processing systems that have dramatically improved their ability to handle large volumes of information. This has allowed the industry to bring the average claim processing time down to 89.5 days. For example, the firm Noridian used technology to enable operators to process four to five times more claims in the same amount of time as under their old system, and to speed the form retrieval process for better customer service.

The VA has proposed a more typically governmental solution of adding 1000 more claims adjudicators. Even apart from the cost of $80 million or so of adding these personnel, the question is whether adding additional personnel to a cumbersome system is the best possible way to speed up transactions and improve service. A better idea would be to expand the Vet Centers to offer some assistance in helping veterans figure out their disability claims. The 1000 claims experts could be placed inside the Vet Centers (5 per center), thus enabling veterans and their families to obtain quick assistance for many routine claims. Vet Centers would only require minor modifications (secure storage space, additional computers and offices) to fill this role.

There has been a tendency in the media to focus on the number of US deaths in Iraq, rather than the volume of wounded, injured, or sick.

The best solution might be to simplify the process—by adopting something closer to the way the IRS [Internal Revenue Service] deals with tax returns. The VBA could simply approve all veterans' claims as they are filed—at least to a certain minimum level—and then audit a sample of them to weed out and deter fraudulent claims. At present, nearly 90 percent of claims are approved. VBA claims specialists could then be redeployed to assist veterans in making claims, especially at VA's "Vet Centers." This startlingly easy switch would ensure that the US no longer leaves disabled veterans to fend for themselves. . . .

Support for the Survivors

There has been a tendency in the media to focus on the number of US deaths in Iraq, rather than the volume of wounded, injured, or sick. This may have led the public to underestimate the deadliness and long-term impact of the war on civilian society and the government's pocketbook. Were it not for modern medical advances and better body armor, we would have suffered even more loss of life. . . .

If . . . Congress really wants to support our troops, it should start by spending a few more pennies on the ones who have already fought and come home.

8

The VA Is Prepared to Meet the Long-Term Care Needs of Returning Vets

Patricia Vandenberg

Patricia Vandenberg is the assistant deputy undersecretary for health for policy and planning at the U.S. Department of Veterans Affairs.

The U.S. Department of Veterans Affairs (VA) readily acknowledges the changing long-term health care needs of veterans. To address those needs, VA has prioritized care for veterans most in need. Accordingly, it is expanding both the services it provides as well as those it purchases from community providers. It has coordinated benefits with Medicare, Medicaid, State Veterans Homes, and private insurance in order to provide comprehensive and compassionate high-quality care. The VA is adapting its services to meet the unique needs of today's returning veterans by providing "Internet cafes," computer games and videos, and overnight family visits in residential care facilities.

I would like to take this opportunity to give an overview of VA's long-term care services and programs.

VA has testified [before Congress] previously that there is a great and growing need for long-term care services for elderly and disabled veterans. Between 2005 and 2012, the number of enrolled veterans aged 65 and older is projected to increase from 3.45 million to 3.92 million. The number of

Patricia Vandenberg, Statement before the House Committee on Veterans Affairs, Subcommittee on Health, May 9, 2007.

enrolled veterans aged 85 and older will increase from 337,000 to 741,000 during the same period. This latter group, those aged 85 and older, are the most vulnerable of the older veteran population and are especially likely to require not only long-term care services, but also other health care services along the continuum of care, such as acute care and preventive care.

Addressing the Most Critical Needs

VA is addressing the mandates for nursing home care for service-connected veterans with a disability rated at seventy percent or greater and veterans who need nursing home care for their service-connected disability and for selected home- and community-based care services for all enrolled veterans, as set by Congress in the Veterans Millennium Health Care and Benefits Act, Public Law 106-117, and prioritizing care for those veterans most in need of our services including:

- veterans returning from Operation Enduring Freedom [in Afghanistan] and Operation Iraqi Freedom (OEF/OIF) service,

- veterans with service-connected disabilities,

- veterans with lower incomes, and

- veterans with special health care needs such as serious chronic mental illness and spinal cord injury and disease

---

VA health care providers work closely with patients and family, on a case-by-case basis, to coordinate the veteran's various Federal and State benefits, and to maximize options for that veteran.

Since many enrolled veterans are also eligible for long-term care through other public and private programs, including Medicare, Medicaid, State Veterans Homes, and private insurance, it is in the interest of both the government and veterans to coordinate the benefits of their various programs and work together toward the goal of providing compassionate, and high-quality care. VA staff have extensive experience in coordinating services among agencies for the benefit of veterans, within statutory limitations and in accordance with desires of patients and their families. I want to emphasize that our efforts in long-term care case management are driven by the clinical needs of each patient, the patient's preferences, and the benefit options available to that patient. VA health care providers work closely with patients and family, on a case-by-case basis, to coordinate the veteran's various Federal and State benefits, and to maximize options for that veteran. Among those programs within VA that address coordinating veteran care needs are Social Work Service, Home Based Primary Care Program, community health nurse coordinators, and Care Coordination/Telehealth.

VA's philosophy of care, in keeping with practice patterns throughout the public and private sectors, is to provide patient-centered long-term care services in the least restrictive setting that is suitable for a veteran's medical condition and personal circumstances, and whenever possible, in home and community-based settings. This approach honors veterans' preferences at the end of life and helps to maintain relationships with the veteran's spouse, family, friends, faith and community. Nursing home care should be reserved for situations in which the veteran can no longer be safely maintained in the home and community. VA long-term care is composed of a dynamic array of services provided in residential, outpatient, and inpatient settings that can be deployed as needed to meet a veteran's changing health care needs over time. In addition to direct patient care services, VA supports important research and education related to the health care needs of elderly and disabled veterans through the work of its 21 Geriatric Research, Education, and Clinical Centers, or GRECCs.

Non-institutional Care

VA's strategic goal is to make non-institutional long-term care services available to every enrolled veteran who needs them and seeks them from VA. The spectrum of non-institutional home and community-based long-term care services supported by VA includes:

- Home Based Primary Care,

- Contract Skilled Home Care,

- Homemaker/Home Health Aide,

- Adult Day Health Care,

- Home Respite,

- Home Hospice,

- Spinal Cord Injury Home Care, and

- Care Coordination/Home Telehealth

VA also provides quality oversight of care purchased by veterans in Community Residential Care and Medical Foster Home facilities through an annual review process and monthly or more frequent monitoring by VA staff.

The workload in the non-institutional care programs included in Long-Term Care has grown from an average daily census of 19,810 in 1998 to 29,489 through the end of FY [fiscal year] 2006. More than 9 out of 10 VA Medical Centers now offer some or all of these services, substantially enhancing veterans' access to non-institutional long-term care services. VA continues to have a VISN [Veterans Integrated Service Network] performance measure to increase the average daily census of veterans receiving home and community-based care. Each VISN has been assigned targets for increase in their non-institutional long-term care workload. VA is expanding both the services it provides directly and those it purchases from providers in the community.

Innovations in Long-Term Care

VA expects to meet a substantial part of the growing need for long-term care through such innovative services as Care Coordination/Home Telehealth. Care Coordination in VA involves the use of health informatics; telehealth and disease management technologies to enhance and extend existing care; and case management activities. VA's national Care Coordination initiative commenced in 2003 and is supported by a national program office. Care Coordination enables appropriately selected veteran patients with chronic conditions such as diabetes and congestive heart failure to remain in their own homes, and it defers or obviates the need for long-term institutional care. Care Coordination services are linked not only with services for the elderly such as Home Based Primary Care, but also with other services including Mental Health Intensive Case Management and General Primary and Ambulatory Care. Care Coordination/Home Telehealth enables delivery of VA health care to veterans living remotely from VA medical facilities, including those in rural areas.

Transforming the culture of care in nursing homes from the traditional medical model to a more home-like, patient-centered model is an important initiative in all of our nursing home programs.

Inevitably, some veterans will be unable to continue to live safely in the community and will require nursing home care. VA will continue to provide nursing home care for all veterans for whom such care is mandated by statute, who need such care and seek it from VA. In addition, VA will continue to provide post-acute care for veterans who have suffered an accident or illness such as a broken hip or stroke, who require a period of recovery and rehabilitation before returning to the community. VA will also continue to provide nursing home care for veterans with special needs, including those with spinal cord injury or disease, ventilator dependence, and serious chronic mental illness. VA expects to sustain existing capacity in its own Nursing Home Care Units and in the Community Nursing Home Program and to support continued expansion of capacity in the State Veterans Home Program. Transforming the culture of care in nursing homes from the traditional medical model to a more home-like, patient-centered model is an important initiative in all of our nursing home programs.

State Veterans Homes

VA's State Veterans Home Program assists states in providing care to veterans in State Veterans Homes. Veterans' eligibility for each state's program is determined by the individual state using the state's own criteria. There are State Veterans Homes in operation or under construction in all 50 states and Puerto Rico. VA supports construction and renovation of State Veterans Homes through the State Home Construction Grant Program, which provides matching funds to assist states in purchasing, constructing, and renovating properties to serve as nursing homes, domiciliaries, and adult day health care centers. Projects are funded in priority order until available funds for each fiscal year are exhausted, with highest priority given to renovation projects needed to correct life safety deficiencies and for construction of new capacity in geographic areas of need.

The second component of the State Veterans Home is the Per Diem Program. VA pays a per diem to assist the states in providing care for eligible veteran residents. Recently, Public Law 109-461, Section 211, provided VA authority to pay State Veterans Homes the prevailing rate or the home's daily cost of care, whichever is less, for veterans in need of such care for a service-connected disability and for veterans who have a service-connected disability rated at 70 percent or more. VA is currently in the process of developing regulations to implement the provisions of this authority.

Thirdly, we provide medication at VA expense to eligible veterans residing in State Veterans Homes.

The fourth component of the State Veterans Home program is VA's oversight function. VA has developed a system of on-site inspections to assure quality of care in State Veterans Homes, including the identification of life safety issues.

The VA Deputy Secretary charged a VA Task Force to explore opportunities for State Veterans Homes to provide non-institutional care for veterans. The Task Force solicited the views of representatives of the State Veterans Homes and State Departments of Veterans Affairs, who indicated that the most important need is to lower barriers to their participation in the Adult Day Health Care program. VA will revise the regulations for the State Home Adult Day Health Care program accordingly. Also, VA increases the per diem payment for this program annually, which should encourage greater participation by the states. VA staff responsible for the State Home Program communicate frequently with State Veterans Home and State Department of Veterans Affairs personnel to answer questions, share information, and solicit stakeholder input on VA policies and programs.

Looking to the Future

The total FY 2008 budget request for long-term care is $4.6 billion, of which 90 percent will support institutional services and 10 percent non-institutional home and community-based care. This request will provide the resources necessary for VA to strengthen our position as a leader in providing high-quality services for a growing population of elderly disabled veterans, as well as those veterans returning from service in OEF/OIF, veterans with service-connected disabilities, veterans with lower incomes, and veterans with special health care needs. As you know, the population of veterans who are enrolled for health care in the VA are, on average, older, poorer, and sicker than the general population. VA is already seeing the kinds of demographic changes that are projected for the nation as a whole in coming decades. Recently, VA has also begun to care for younger veterans who have sustained polytraumatic injuries during their service in Operation Enduring Freedom and Operation Iraqi Freedom. While the number of seriously disabled OEF/OIF veterans is relatively small, compared to the total number of veterans requiring extended care services, the complexity of care they require is high and their personal and social needs differ from those of older veterans. VA is moving to adapt its long-term care services to meet the needs of all veterans.

Many returning veterans are presenting with multiple and severe disabilities, including speech, hearing and visual impairment as well as loss of limbs and brain injuries, and behavioral issues due to the stress of combat.

Many returning veterans are presenting with multiple and severe disabilities, including speech, hearing and visual impairment as well as loss of limbs and brain injuries, and behavioral issues due to the stress of combat. In addition, they have families, including children, who want to be actively involved in their care. Unlike other cohorts of veterans in long-term care, this cohort thrives on independence, is physically strong, and is part of a generation socialized differently than their older counterparts. These generational differences pose unique challenges in the institutional and long-term care environment.

VA is taking measures to first recognize the generational differences of this population and incorporate them into the care routines. For example, in VA nursing homes, transforming the culture of care to make the living space more home friendly is important, as is having an "internet café", computer games, or age appropriate music and videos available for nursing home residents. Allowing for family, especially children, to visit and perhaps even stay over when needed is another example of accommodating generational differences. Personalizing care routines such as bathing and dining times and offering food items that are palatable to younger persons are examples of the changes that are occurring in long-term care.

VA takes great pride in our accomplishments, and looks forward ... to continu[ing] the Department's tradition of providing timely, high-quality health care to those who have helped defend and preserve freedom around the world.

9

The Veterans Health Care System Is a Poor Model for Private Health Care

Richard E. Ralston

Richard E. Ralston is the executive director of Americans for Free Choice in Medicine.

Proponents of nationalized medicine have often cited the Veterans Administration as the model of efficiency and quality care as demonstrated by the government; however, veterans are subjected to treatment delays, bungled bureaucracy, and deplorable structural and living conditions. Such flaws suggest that Americans would be unwise to embrace the idea of a national health care system. The federal government first needs to clean up its own health care programs before contemplating the takeover of private citizens' health care.

For years the advocates of a total takeover of health care by the government have pointed to the Veterans Administration as the model of efficient and caring health care by our government. It provides an ideal model, they said, for all health care. They must have forgotten to tell us to pay no attention to the leaks, the pealing paint and the rats in the corner while they push to eliminate personal choice for everyone and trap us all in a system with no options and nowhere else to go.

Richard E. Ralston, "Should the Veterans Administration Take Over All Health Care?" *Capitalism Magazine*, March 18, 2007. Americans for Free Choice in Medicine, www.afcm.org. Copyright © 2007. All rights reserved. Reproduced by permission. http://www.capmag.com/article.asp?ID=4937.

For whom should we expect the government to provide the best health care treatment—and living conditions while that care is delivered—if not for those who have fulfilled their duty to that government: our wounded combat veterans? They expect (and should demand) the best treatment possible. Yet, wounded veterans are constrained to a system with few or no choice of options. What, then, should the rest of us expect from the loving arms and warm embrace of government-managed health care? What would happen if we were all involuntarily absorbed into the bosom of government health care? Would we expect tender and solicitous care—or a distant, insensitive, wasteful and indifferent bureaucracy?

The tireless advocates of medical socialism will continue to maintain that only the government can care for us adequately.

A Poor Track Record

Both the U.S. Army and the Veterans Administration clearly have large numbers of competent medical professionals delivering care. But soldiers in rehabilitation often have to wait a long time, travel a long way or live in terrible conditions to receive care. One of the amazing things about the problems at Walter Reed [Army Medical Center in Washington, D.C.] was that only the government could have developed the idea of a live-in, out-patient clinic.

In the face of this calamity and such inspirations as the tired response of all levels of government to Hurricane Katrina, the tireless advocates of medical socialism will continue to maintain that only the government can care for us adequately.

In the face of New York's cartel of hospital administrators and health care public employee unions driving the annual cost of New York Medicaid past $47 billion and clamoring for more, the friends of ever-growing government will tell us that they will always manage spending better than private providers.

The Reality of the Situation

When we encounter those from this fantasy world of supposedly caring and efficient government, we must always respond with the facts. When someone says that the problem with health care is the cost and only the government can restrain expense, we must always ask them exactly when the government developed an ability to restrain expense. During the forty years of exploding Medicare and Medicaid spending? Or while the gross waste and fraud in New York Medicaid was going into orbit?

A government drawing on unlimited taxes and debt cannot control costs or even fraud.

When we are told that health care by for-profit companies should be outlawed because such profits increase our health care costs, we must respond that it is the need to make a profit that results in what cost control we have. A government drawing on unlimited taxes and debt cannot control costs or even fraud. And what kind of "profit" will the leaders of public employee unions—and the politicians they fund—gain if they seize a total monopoly over health care and eliminate all of our other options?

When we are told that we would not have to worry about paying for our health care—whatever it costs—because the government will pick up the tab, we need to point out that once everything is "free" it will get really expensive. And we will watch the government decide that it owns what it is paying for—and that it therefore owns our bodies and can instruct us what to do with them.

But it will still be a free country, right?

Before engaging in such debates, we must first tell the government to get health care in order and under control for those who have been wounded in government service. In light of their ongoing failure to get that right, however, we should not tolerate even the request to give government more power.

10

Private Health Care Could Learn Much from the Veterans Health Care System

Phillip Longman

Phillip Longman is a Schwartz Senior Fellow at the New America Foundation and the author of The Empty Cradle.

For many people, the thought of veterans hospitals conjures up images of shabby, unsanitary facilities wallowing in budgetary scandal. In fact, today's veterans facilities are state-of-the-industry not only in structural and equipment considerations, but also in technical and professional expertise. There are several reasons for this new efficiency in veterans facilities. Unlike Medicare, the Veterans Health Administration (VHA) can negotiate for deep discounts with private contractors and pharmaceutical manufacturers. Moreover, its sheer size and membership affords it discounted costs. In addition, the VHA typically has a life-long relationship with its patients and therefore a powerful incentive to prevent and effectively manage disease. The private health care system can learn many lessons from the VHA.

Quick. When you read "veterans hospital," what comes to mind? Maybe you recall the headlines from a dozen years ago about the three decomposed bodies found near a veterans medical center in Salem, Va. Two turned out to be the remains of patients who had wandered off months before. The other

Phillip Longman, "The Best Care Anywhere," *The Washington Monthly*, vol. 37, January/February 2005, pp. 38–48. Copyright 2005 by Washington Monthly Publishing, LLC, 733 15th St. NW, Suite 520, Washington DC 20005. (202) 393-5155. Web site: www.washingtonmonthly.com. Reproduced by permission.

body had been resting in place for more than 15 years. The Veterans Health Administration (VHA) admitted that its search for the missing patients had been "cursory."

Or maybe you recall images from movies like *Born on the Fourth of July*, in which Tom Cruise plays a wounded Vietnam vet who becomes radicalized by his shabby treatment in a crumbling, rat-infested veterans hospital in the Bronx. Sample dialogue: "This place is a f---in' slum!"

By the mid-1990s, the reputation of veterans hospitals had sunk so low that conservatives routinely used their example as a kind of reductio ad absurdum critique of any move toward "socialized medicine." Here, for instance, is Jarret B. Wollstein, a right-wing activist/author, railing against the [President Bill] Clinton health-care plan in 1994: "To see the future of health care in America for you and your children under Clinton's plan," Wollstein warned, "just visit any Veterans Administration [VA] hospital. You'll find filthy conditions, shortages of everything, and treatment bordering on barbarism."

And so it goes today. If the debate is over health-care reform, it won't be long before some free-market conservative will jump up and say that the sorry shape of the nation's veterans hospitals just proves what happens when government gets into the health-care business. And if he's a true believer, he'll then probably go on to suggest, quoting [*New York Times* pundit] William Safire and other free marketers, that the government should just shut down the whole miserable system and provide veterans with health-care vouchers.

Yet here's a curious fact that few conservatives or liberals know. Who do you think receives higher-quality health care. Medicare patients who are free to pick their own doctors and specialists? Or aging veterans stuck in those presumably filthy VA hospitals with their antiquated equipment, uncaring administrators, and incompetent staff? An answer came in 2003, when the prestigious *New England Journal of Medicine* published a study that compared veterans health facilities on 11 measures of quality with fee-for-service Medicare. On all 11 measures, the quality of care in veterans facilities proved to be "significantly better."

Here's another curious fact. The *Annals of Internal Medicine* published a study that compared veterans health facilities with commercial managed-care systems in their treatment of diabetes patients. In seven out of seven measures of quality, the VA provided better care.

In every single category, the VHA system outperforms the highest rated non-VHA hospitals.

It gets stranger. Pushed by large employers who are eager to know what they are buying when they purchase health care for their employees, an outfit called the National Committee for Quality Assurance [NCQA] today ranks health-care plans on 17 different performance measures. These include how well the plans manage high blood pressure or how precisely they adhere to standard protocols of evidence-based medicine such as prescribing beta blockers for patients recovering from a heart attack. Winning NCQA's seal of approval is the gold standard in the health-care industry. And who do you suppose [2005's] winner is: Johns Hopkins? Mayo Clinic? Massachusetts General? Nope. In every single category, the VHA system outperforms the highest rated non-VHA hospitals.

Not convinced? Consider what vets themselves think. Sure, it's not hard to find vets who complain about difficulties in establishing eligibility. Many are outraged that the [George W.] Bush administration has decided to deny previously promised health-care benefits to veterans who don't have service-related illnesses or who can't meet a strict means test. Yet these grievances are about access to the system, not about the quality of care received by those who get in. Veterans groups tenaciously defend the VHA and applaud its turnaround. "The quality of care is outstanding," says Peter Gayton, deputy director for veterans affairs and rehabilitation at the American Legion. In the latest independent survey, 81 percent of VHA hospital patients express satisfaction with the care they receive, compared to 77 percent of Medicare and Medicaid patients.

Outside experts agree that the VHA has become an industry leader in its safety and quality measures. Dr. Donald M. Berwick, president of the Institute for Health Care Improvement and one of the nation's top health-care quality experts, praises the VHA's information technology as "spectacular." The venerable Institute of Medicine notes that the VHA's "integrated health information system, including its framework for using performance measures to improve quality, is considered one of the best in the nation."

How and why the VHA became the benchmark for quality medicine . . . suggests that much of what we think we know about health care . . . is just wrong.

Rethinking the Health-Care Model

If this gives you cognitive dissonance, it should. The story of how and why the VHA became the benchmark for quality medicine in the United States suggests that much of what we think we know about health care and medical economics is just wrong. It's natural to believe that more competition and consumer choice in health care would lead to greater quality and lower costs, because in almost every other realm, it does. That's why the Bush administration—which has been promoting greater use of information technology and other quality improvement in health care—also wants to give individuals new tax-free "health savings accounts" and high-deductible insurance plans. Together, these measures are supposed to encourage patients to do more comparison shopping and haggling with their doctors; therefore, they create more market discipline in the system.

But when it comes to health care, it's a government bureaucracy that's setting the standard for maintaining best practices while reducing costs, and it's the private sector that's lagging in quality. That unexpected reality needs examining if we're to have any hope of understanding what's wrong with America's health-care system and how to fix it. It turns out that precisely because the VHA is a big, government-run system that has nearly a lifetime relationship with its patients, it has incentives for investing in quality and keeping its patients well—incentives that are lacking in for-profit medicine. . . .

Getting Lost in the System

To understand the larger lessons of the VHA's turnaround, it's necessary to pause for a moment to think about what comprises quality health care. The first criterion likely to come to mind is the presence of doctors who are highly trained, committed professionals. They should know a lot about biochemistry, anatomy, cellular and molecular immunology, and other details about how the human body works—and have the academic credentials to prove it. As it happens, the VHA has long had many doctors who answer to that description. Indeed, most VHA doctors have faculty appointments with academic hospitals.

Doctors aren't the only ones who define the quality of your health care. There are also many other people involved.

But when you get seriously sick, it's not just one doctor who will be involved in your care. These days, chances are you'll see many doctors, including different specialists. Therefore, how well these doctors communicate with one another and work as a team matters a lot. "Forgetfulness is such a constant problem in the system," says [Dr. Donald] Berwick of the Institute for Health Care Improvement. "It doesn't remember you. Doesn't remember that you were here and here and then there. It doesn't remember your story."

Are all your doctors working from the same medical record and making entries that are clearly legible? Do they have a reliable system to ensure that no doctor will prescribe drugs that will interact harmfully with medications prescribed by another doctor? Is any one of them going to take responsibility for coordinating your care so that, for example, you don't leave the hospital without the right follow-up medication or knowing how and when to take it? Just about anyone who's had a serious illness, or tried to be an advocate for a sick loved one, knows that all too often the answer is no.

Doctors aren't the only ones who define the quality of your health care. There are also many other people involved— nurses, pharmacists, lab technicians, orderlies, even custodians. Any one of these people could kill you if they were to do their jobs wrong. Even a job as lowly as changing a bedpan, if not done right, can spread a deadly infection throughout a hospital. Each of these people is part of an overall system of care, and if the system lacks cohesion and quality control, many people will be injured and many will die. . . .

Now, you might ask, what's so hard about preventing these kinds of fatal lapses in health care? The airline industry, after all, also requires lots of complicated teamwork and potentially dangerous technology, but it doesn't wind up killing hundreds of thousands of its customers each year. Indeed, airlines, even when in bankruptcy, continuously improve their safety records. By contrast, the death toll from medical errors alone is equivalent to a fully loaded jumbo-jet crashing each day.

Improving Medicine Through Technology

Why doesn't this change? Well, much of it has changed in the veterans health-care system, where advanced information technology today serves not only to deeply reduce medical errors, but also to improve diagnoses and implement coordinated, evidence-based care. Or at least so I kept reading in the professional literature on health-care quality in the United States. I arranged to visit the VA Medical Center in Washington, D.C., to see what all these experts were so excited about.

The complex's main building is a sprawling, imposing structure located three miles north of the Capitol building. When it was built in 1972, it was in the heart of Washington's ghetto, a neighborhood dangerous enough that one nurse I spoke with remembered having to lock her car doors and drive as fast as she could down Irving Street when she went home at night.

While history is everywhere in [the Washington, D.C., VA Medical Center], it is also among the most advanced, modern health-care facilities on the globe.

Today, the surrounding area is rapidly gentrifying. And the medical center has evolved, too. Certain sights, to be sure, remind you of how alive the past still is here. In its nursing home facility, there are still a few veterans of World War I. Standing outside of the hospital's main entrance, I was moved by the sight of two elderly gentlemen, both standing at near attention, and sporting neatly pressed Veterans of Foreign Wars dress caps with MIA/POW [missing in action/prisoner of war] insignias. One turned out to be a survivor of the Bataan Death March.

But while history is everywhere in this hospital, it is also among the most advanced, modern health-care facilities on the globe—a place that hosts an average of four visiting foreign delegations a week. The hospital has a spacious generic lobby with a food court, ATM machines, and a gift shop. But once you are in the wards, you notice something very different: doctors and nurses wheeling bed tables with wireless laptops attached down the corridors. How does this change the practice of medicine? Opening up his laptop, Dr. Ross Fletcher, an avuncular, white-haired cardiologist who led the hospital's adoption of information technology, begins a demonstration.

With a key stroke, Dr. Fletcher pulls up the medical records for one of his current patients—an 87-year-old veteran living in Montgomery County, Md. Normally, sharing such records with a reporter or anyone else would, of course, be highly unethical and illegal, but the patient, Dr. Fletcher explains, has given him permission.

Software Program Aids Diagnosis

Soon it becomes obvious why this patient feels that getting the word out about the VHA's information technology is important. Up pops a chart showing a daily record of his weight as it has fluctuated over a several-month period. The data for this chart, Dr. Fletcher explains, flows automatically from a special scale the patient uses in his home that sends a wireless signal to a modem.

Why is the chart important? Because it played a key role, Fletcher explains, in helping him to make a difficult diagnosis. While recovering from Lyme Disease and a hip fracture, the patient began periodically complaining of shortness of breath. Chest X-rays were ambiguous and confusing. They showed something amiss in one lung, but not the other, suggesting possible lung cancer. But Dr. Fletcher says he avoided having to chase down that possibility when he noticed a pattern jumping out of the graph generated from the patient's scale at home.

The chart clearly showed that the patient gained weight around the time he experienced shortness of breath. This pattern, along with the record of the hip fracture, helped Dr. Fletcher to form a hypothesis that turned out to be accurate. A buildup of fluid in the patient's lung was causing him to gain weight. The fluid gathered only in one lung because the patient was consistently sleeping on one side to cope with the pain from his hip fracture. The fluid in the lung indicated that the patient was in immediate need of treatment for congestive heart failure, and, fortunately, he received it in time.

Safeguarding Against Medical Error

The same software program, known as VistA, also plays a key role in preventing medical errors. Kay J. Craddock, who spent most of her 28 years with the VHA as a nurse, and who today coordinates the use of the information systems at the VA Medical Center, explains how. In the old days, pharmacists did their best to decipher doctors' handwritten prescription orders, while nurses, she says, did their best to keep track of which patients should receive which medicines by shuffling 3-by-5 cards.

Today, by contrast, doctors enter their orders into their laptops. The computer system immediately checks any order against the patient's records. If the doctors working with a patient have prescribed an inappropriate combination of medicines or overlooked the patient's previous allergic reaction to a drug, the computer sends up a red flag. Later, when hospital pharmacists fill those prescriptions, the computer system generates a bar code that goes on the bottle or intravenous bag and registers what the medicine is, who it is for, when it should be administered, in what dose, and by whom.

Each patient also has an ID bracelet with its own bar code, and so does each nurse. Before administering any drug, a nurse must first scan the patient's ID bracelet, then her own, and then the barcode on the medicine. If she has the wrong patient or the wrong medicine, the computer will tell her. The computer will also create a report if she's late in administering a dose, "and saying you were just too busy is not an excuse," says Craddock. . . .

Better Efficiency and Access

In speaking with several of the young residents at the VA Medical Center, I realized that the computer system is also a great aid to efficiency. At the university hospitals where they had also trained, said the residents, they constantly had to run around trying to retrieve records—first upstairs to get X-rays from the radiology department, then downstairs to pick up lab results. By contrast, when making their rounds at the VA Medical Center, they just flip open their laptops when they enter a patient's room. In an instant, they can see not only all of the patient's latest data, but also a complete medical record going back as far as the mid-1980s, including records of care performed in any other VHA hospital or clinic.

Anyone enrolled in the VHA [is] able to access his or her own complete medical records from a home computer, or give permission for others to do so.

Along with the obvious benefits this brings in making diagnoses, it also means that residents don't face impossibly long hours dealing with paperwork. "It lets these twentysomethings go home in time to do the things twentysomethings like to do," says Craddock. One neurologist practicing at both Georgetown University Hospital and the VA Medical Center reports that he can see as many patients in a few hours at the veterans hospital as he can all day at Georgetown.

By [summer 2005], anyone enrolled in the VHA will be able to access his or her own complete medical records from a home computer, or give permission for others to do so. "Think what this means," says Dr. Robert M. Kolodner, acting chief health informatics officer for the VHA. "Say you're living on the West Coast, and you call up your aging dad back East. You ask him to tell you what his doctor said during his last visit and he mumbles something about taking a blue pill and white one. [Now], you'll be able to monitor his medical record, and know exactly what pills he is supposed to be taking."

The same system reminds doctors to prescribe appropriate care for patients when they leave the hospital, such as beta blockers for heart attack victims, or eye exams for diabetics. It also keeps track of which vets are due for a flu shot, a breast cancer screen, or other follow-up care—a task virtually impossible to pull off using paper records. Another benefit of electronic records became apparent when the drug-maker Merck announced a recall of its popular arthritis medication, Vioxx. The VHA was able to identify which of its patients were on the drug within minutes, and to switch them to less dangerous substitutes within days.

Similarly, in the midst of a nationwide shortage of flu vaccine, the system has also allowed the VHA to identify, almost instantly, those veterans who are in greatest need of a flu shot and to make sure those patients have priority....

The VistA system also helps to put more science into the practice of medicine. For example, electronic medical records collectively form a powerful database that enables researchers to look back and see which procedures work best without having to assemble and rifle through innumerable paper records. This database also makes it possible to discover emerging disease vectors quickly and effectively. For example, when a veterans hospital in Kansas City noticed an outbreak of a rare form of pneumonia among its patients, its computer system quickly spotted the problem: All the patients had been treated with what turned out to be the same bad batch of nasal spray.

Developed at taxpayer expense, the VistA program is available for free to anyone who cares to download it off the Internet. The link is to a demo, but the complete software is nonetheless available.... Not surprisingly, it is currently being used by public health care systems in Finland, Germany, and Nigeria. There is even an Arabic language version up and running in Egypt. Yet VHA officials say they are unaware of any private health care system in the United States that uses the software. Instead, most systems are still drowning in paper, or else just starting to experiment with far more primitive information technologies....

Additional Quality Checks

Obviously, in the VHA system, scanning the patient's ID bracelet and the surgical orders helps, but even that isn't foolproof.
Drawing on his previous experience as a NASA astronaut and
accident investigator, the VHA's safety director, Dr. James
Bagian, has developed a five-step process that VHA surgical
teams now use to verify both the identity of the patient and
where they are supposed to operate. Though it's similar to the
check lists astronauts go through before blast off, it is hardly
rocket science. The most effective part of the drill, says Bagian,
is simply to ask the patient, in language he can understand,
who he is and what he's in for. Yet the efficacy of this and
other simple quality-control measures adopted by the VHA
makes one wonder all the more why the rest of the health-
care system is so slow to follow.

Why Quality Matters

Here's one big reason. As Lawrence P. Casalino, a professor of
public health at the University of Chicago, puts it, "The U.S.
medical market as presently constituted simply does not provide a strong business case for quality.". . .

For health-care providers outside the VHA system, improving quality rarely makes financial sense. Yes, a hospital
may have a business case for purchasing the latest, most expensive imaging devices. The machines will help attract lots of
highly-credentialed doctors to the hospital who will bring lots
of patients with them. The machines will also induce lots of
new demand for hospital services by picking up all sorts of
so-called "pseudo-diseases." These are obscure, symptomless
conditions, like tiny, slow-growing cancers, that patients would
never have otherwise become aware of because they would
have long since died of something else. If you're a fee-for-
service health-care provider, investing in technology that leads
to more treatment of pseudo-disease is a financial no-brainer.

But investing in any technology that ultimately serves to reduce hospital admissions, like an electronic medical record system that enables more effective disease management and reduces medical errors, is likely to take money straight from the bottom line. "The business case for safety . . . remains inadequate . . . [for] the task," concludes Robert Wachter, M.D., in a recent study for Health Affairs in which he surveyed quality control efforts across the U.S. health-care system.

Purchasers of health care usually don't know, and often don't care, about its quality, and so private health-care providers can't increase their incomes by offering it.

If health care was like a more pure market, in which customers know the value of what they are buying, a business case for quality might exist more often. But purchasers of health care usually don't know, and often don't care, about its quality, and so private health-care providers can't increase their incomes by offering it. To begin with, most people don't buy their own health care; their employers do. Consortiums of large employers may have the staff and the market power necessary to evaluate the quality of health-care plans and to bargain for greater commitments to patient safety and evidence-based medicine. And a few actually do so. But most employers are not equipped for this. Moreover, in these days of rapid turnover and vanishing post-retirement health-care benefits, few employers have any significant financial interest in their workers' long-term health.

That's why you don't see many employers buying insurance that covers smoking cessation programs or the various expensive drugs that can help people to quit the habit. If they did, they'd be buying more years of healthy life per dollar than just about any other way they could use their money. But most of the savings resulting from reduced lung cancer, stroke, and heart attacks would go to future employers of their workers, and so such a move makes little financial sense. . . .

What Makes the VA Different

So what's left? Consider why, ultimately, the veterans health system is such an outlier in its commitment to quality. Partly it's because of timely, charismatic leadership. A quasi-military culture may also facilitate acceptance of new technologies and protocols. But there are also other important, underlying factors.

First, unlike virtually all other health-care systems in the United States, VHA has a near lifetime relationship with its patients. Its customers don't jump from one health plan to the next every few years. They start a relationship with the VHA as early as their teens, and it endures. That means that the VHA actually has an incentive to invest in prevention and more effective disease management. When it does so, it isn't just saving money for somebody else. It's maximizing its own resources.

The system's doctors are salaried, which also makes a difference. Most could make more money doing something else, so their commitment to their profession most often derives from a higher-than-usual dose of idealism. Moreover, because they are not profit maximizers, they have no need to be fearful of new technologies or new protocols that keep people well. Nor do they have an incentive to clamor for high-tech devices that don't improve the system's quality or effectiveness of care.

And, because it is a well-defined system, the VHA can act like one. It can systematically attack patient safety issues. It can systematically manage information using standard platforms and interfaces. It can systematically develop and implement evidence-based standards of care. It can systematically discover where its care needs improvement and take corrective measures. In short, it can do what the rest of the health-care sector can't seem to, which is to pursue quality systematically without threatening its own financial viability.

A Proposal for the Future

Hmm. That gives me an idea. No one knows how we're ever going to provide health care for all these aging baby boomers. Meanwhile, in the absence of any near-term major wars, the population of veterans in the United States will fall dramatically in the next decade. Instead of shuttering under-utilized VHA facilities, maybe we should build more. What if we expanded the veterans health-care system and allowed anyone who is either already a vet or who agrees to perform two years of community service a chance to buy in? Indeed, what if we said to young and middle-aged people, if you serve your community and your country, you can make your parents or other loved ones eligible for care in an expanded VHA system?

The system runs circles around Medicare in both cost and quality. Unlike Medicare, it's allowed by law to negotiate for deep drug discounts, and does. Unlike Medicare, it provides long-term nursing home care. And it demonstrably delivers some of the best, if not the best, quality health care in the United States with amazing efficiency. Between 1999 and 2003, the number of patients enrolled in the VHA system increased by 70 percent, yet funding (not adjusted for inflation) increased by only 41 percent. So the VHA has not only become the health care industry's best quality performer, it has done so while spending less and less on each patient. Decreasing cost and improving quality go hand and hand in industries like autos and computers—but in health care, such a relationship is virtually unheard of. The more people we can get into the VHA, the more efficient and effective the American health-care system will be.

We could start with demonstration projects using VHA facilities that are currently under-utilized or slated to close. [In May 2004], the VHA announced it was closing hospitals in

Pittsburgh; Gulfport, Miss.; and Brecksville, Ohio. Even after the closures, the VHA will still have more than 4 million square feet of vacant or obsolete real estate. Beyond this, there are empty facilities available from bankrupt HMOs [health maintenance organizations] and public hospitals, such as the defunct D.C. General. Let the VHA take over these facilities, and apply its state-of-the-art information systems, safety systems, and protocols of evidence-based medicine.

Once fully implemented, the plan would allow Americans to avoid skipping from one health-care plan to the next over their lifetimes, with all the discontinuities in care and record keeping and disincentives to preventative care that this entails. No matter where you moved in the country, or how often you changed jobs, or where you might happen to come down with an illness, there would be a VHA facility nearby where your complete medical records would be available and the same evidence-based protocols of medicine would be practiced.

True Reform Is Possible

You might decide that such a plan is not for you. But, as with mass transit, an expanded VHA would offer you a benefit even if you didn't choose to use it. Just as more people riding commuter trains means fewer cars in your way, more people using the VHA would mean less crowding in your own, private doctor's waiting room, as well as more pressure on your private health-care network to match the VHA's performance on cost and quality.

Why make public service a requirement for receiving VHA care? Because it's in the spirit of what the veterans health-care system is all about. It's not an entitlement; it's recognition for those who serve. America may not need as many soldiers as in the past, but it has more need than ever for people who will volunteer to better their communities.

Would such a system stand in danger of becoming woefully under-funded, just as the current VHA system is today?

Veterans comprise a declining share of the population, and the number of Americans who have personal contact with military life continues to shrink. It is therefore not surprising that veterans health-care issues barely register on the national agenda, even in times of war. But, as with any government benefit, the broader the eligibility, the more political support it is likely to receive. Many veterans will object to the idea of sharing their health care system with non-vets; indeed, many already have issues with the VHA treating vets who do not have combat-related disabilities. But in the long run, extending eligibility to non-vets may be the only way to ensure that more veterans get the care they were promised and deserve.

Does this plan seem too radical? Well, perhaps it does for now. We'll have to let the ranks of the uninsured further swell, let health-care costs consume larger and larger portions of payrolls and household budgets, let more and more Americans die from medical errors and mismanaged care, before any true reform of the health-care system becomes possible. But it is time that our debates over health care took the example of the veterans health-care system into account and tried to learn some lessons from it.

11

Military Doctors Misdiagnose Mental Illness to Save on Costs

Joshua Kors

Joshua Kors is a journalist based in New York.

In the U.S. Army's separations manual is a regulation regarding the discharge from military service of a soldier with a "personality disorder." Although such discharge is an "honorable" discharge, the diagnosis releases the U.S. Department of Veterans Affairs (VA) from having to provide medical care or disability pay to soldiers discharged under this category. Moreover, if a soldier has not served out his enlistment contract upon receiving such a discharge, he must return a part of his re-enlistment bonus. Several soldiers have alleged that some military doctors are withholding this information from discharged soldiers. In fact, there are accusations that doctors actually have encouraged soldiers to accept these discharges and advised soldiers that medical benefits and disability would be paid.

Jon Town has spent the last few years fighting two battles, one against his body, the other against the US Army. Both began in October 2004 in Ramadi, Iraq. He was standing in the doorway of his battalion's headquarters when a 107-millimeter rocket struck two feet above his head. The impact punched a piano-sized hole in the concrete facade, sparked a huge fireball and tossed the 25-year-old Army specialist to the floor, where he lay blacked out among the rubble.

Joshua Kors, "How Specialist Town Lost His Benefits," *The Nation*, April 9, 2007, pp. 11–18. Copyright © 2007 by The Nation Magazine/The Nation Company, Inc. Reproduced by permission.

"The next thing I remember is waking up on the ground." Men from his unit had gathered around his body and were screaming his name. "They started shaking me. But I was numb all over," he says. "And it's weird because . . . because for a few minutes you feel like you're not really there. I could see them, but I couldn't hear them. I couldn't hear anything. I started shaking because I thought I was dead."

Never the Same Again

Eventually the rocket shrapnel was removed from Town's neck and his ears stopped leaking blood. But his hearing never really recovered, and in many ways, neither has his life. A soldier honored twelve times during his seven years in uniform, Town has spent the last three struggling with deafness, memory failure and depression. By September 2006 he and the Army agreed he was no longer combat-ready.

But instead of sending Town to a medical board and discharging him because of his injuries, doctors at Fort Carson, Colorado, did something strange: They claimed Town's wounds were actually caused by a "personality disorder." Town was then booted from the Army and told that under a personality disorder discharge, he would never receive disability or medical benefits.

> *The conditions of their discharge have infuriated many in the military community, including the injured soldiers and their families, veterans' rights groups, even military officials required to process these dismissals.*

Town is not alone. A six-month investigation has uncovered multiple cases in which soldiers wounded in Iraq are suspiciously diagnosed as having a personality disorder, then prevented from collecting benefits. The conditions of their discharge have infuriated many in the military community, including the injured soldiers and their families, veterans' rights groups, even military officials required to process these dismissals.

They say the military is purposely misdiagnosing soldiers like Town and that it's doing so for one reason: to cheat them out of a lifetime of disability and medical benefits, thereby saving billions in expenses.

Regulatory Rationale

In the Army's separations manual it's called Regulation 635-200, Chapter 5–13: "Separation Because of Personality Disorder." It's an alluring choice for a cash-strapped military because enacting it is quick and cheap. The Department of Veterans Affairs doesn't have to provide medical care to soldiers dismissed with personality disorder. That's because under Chapter 5–13, personality disorder is a pre-existing condition. The VA is only required to treat wounds sustained during service.

Soldiers discharged under 5–13 can't collect disability pay either. To receive those benefits, a soldier must be evaluated by a medical board, which must confirm that he is wounded and that his wounds stem from combat. The process takes several months, in contrast with a 5–13 discharge, which can be wrapped up in a few days.

If a soldier dismissed under 5–13 hasn't served out his contract, he has to give back a slice of his re-enlistment bonus as well. That amount is often larger than the soldier's final paycheck. As a result, on the day of their discharge, many injured vets learn that they owe the Army several thousand dollars.

Implicating the Professionals

One military official says doctors at his base are doing more than withholding this information from wounded soldiers; they're actually telling them the opposite: that if they go along with a 5–13, they'll get to keep their bonus and receive disability and medical benefits. The official, who demanded anonymity, handles discharge papers at a prominent Army facility. He says the soldiers he works with know they don't have a personality disorder. "But the doctors are telling them, this will get you out quicker, and the VA will take care of you. To stay out of Iraq, a soldier will take that in a heartbeat. What they don't realize is, those things are lies. The soldiers, they don't read the fine print," he says. "They don't know to ask for a med board. They're taking the word of the doctors. Then they sit down with me and find out what a 5–13 really means—they're shocked."

Russell Terry, founder of the Iraq War Veterans Organization (IWVO), says he's watched this scenario play itself out many times. For more than a year, his veterans' rights group has been receiving calls from distraught soldiers discharged under Chapter 5–13. Most, he says, say their military doctors pushed the personality disorder diagnosis, strained to prove that their problems existed before their service in Iraq and refused to acknowledge evidence of posttraumatic stress disorder (PTSD), traumatic brain injury and physical traumas, which would allow them to collect disability and medical benefits.

"These soldiers are coming home from Iraq with all kinds of problems," Terry says. "They go to the VA for treatment, and they're turned away. They're told, 'No, you have a preexisting condition, something from childhood.'" That leap in logic boils Terry's blood. "Everybody receives a psychological screening when they join the military. What I want to know is, if all these soldiers really did have a severe pre-existing condition, how did they get into the military in the first place?"

Terry says that trying to reverse a 5–13 discharge is a frustrating process. A soldier has to claw through a thicket of paperwork, appeals panels and backstage political dealing, and even with the guidance of an experienced advocate, few are successful. "The 5–13," he says, "it's like a scarlet letter you can't get taken off."

A Growing Problem

In the last six years the Army has diagnosed and discharged more than 5,600 soldiers because of personality disorder, according to the Defense Department. And the numbers keep rising: 805 cases in 2001, 980 cases in 2003, 1,086 from January to November 2006. "It's getting worse and worse every day," says the official who handles discharge papers. "At my office the numbers started out normal. Now it's up to three or four soldiers each day. It's like, suddenly everybody has a personality disorder."

The reason is simple, he says. "They're saving a buck. And they're saving the VA money too. It's all about money."

> *By discharging soldiers [for personality disorders] the military could be saving upwards of $8 billion in disability pay.*

Exactly how much money is difficult to calculate. Defense Department records show that across the entire armed forces, more than 22,500 soldiers have been dismissed due to personality disorder in the last six years. How much those soldiers would have collected in disability pay would have been determined by a medical board, which evaluates just how disabled a veteran is. A completely disabled soldier receives about $44,000 a year. In a recent study on the cost of veterans' benefits for the Iraq and Afghanistan wars, Harvard professor Linda Bilmes estimates an average disability payout of $8,890 per year and a future life expectancy of forty years for soldiers returning from service.

Using those figures, by discharging soldiers under Chapter 5–13, the military could be saving upwards of $8 billion in disability pay. Add to that savings the cost of medical care over the soldiers' lifetimes. Bilmes estimates that each year the VA spends an average of $5,000 in medical care per veteran. Applying those numbers, by discharging 22,500 soldiers because of personality disorder, the military saves $4.5 billion in medical care over their lifetimes.

Detrimental Reliance

Town says Fort Carson psychologist Mark Wexler assured him that he would receive disability benefits, VA medical care and that he'd get to keep his bonus—good news he discussed with Christian Fields and Brandon Murray, two soldiers in his unit at Fort Carson. "We talked about it many times," Murray says. "Jon said the doctor there promised him benefits, and he was happy about it. Who wouldn't be?" Town shared that excitement with his wife, Kristy, shortly after his appointment with Wexler. "He said that Wexler had explained to him that he'd get to keep his benefits," Kristy says, "that the doctor had looked into it, and it was all coming with the chapter he was getting."

In fact, Town would not get disability pay or receive long-term VA medical care. And he would have to give back the bulk of his $15,000 bonus. Returning that money meant Town would leave Fort Carson less than empty-handed: He now owed the Army more than $3,000. "We had this on our heads the whole way, driving home to Ohio," says Town. Wexler made him promises, he says, about what would happen if he went along with the diagnosis. "The final day, we find out, none of it was true. It was a total shock. I felt like I'd been betrayed by the Army."

Wexler denies discussing benefits with Town. In a statement, the psychologist writes, "I have never discussed benefits with my patients as that is not my area of expertise. The only thing I said to Spc. [Specialist] Town was that the Chapter 5–13 is an honorable discharge. . . . I assure you, after over 15 years in my position, both as active duty and now civilian, I don't presume to know all the details about benefits and therefore do not discuss them with my patients."

Wexler's boss, Col. Steven Knorr, chief of the Department of Behavioral Health at Evans Army Hospital, declined to speak about Town's case. When asked if doctors at Fort Carson were assuring patients set for a 5–13 discharge that they'll receive disability benefits and keep their bonuses, Knorr said, "I don't believe they're doing that."

A Misapplied Diagnosis

Interviews with soldiers diagnosed with personality disorder suggest that the military is using the psychological condition as a catch-all diagnosis, encompassing symptoms as diverse as deafness, headaches and schizophrenic delusions. That flies in the face of the Army's own regulations.

According to those regulations, to be classified a personality disorder, a soldier's symptoms had to exist before he joined the military. And they have to match the "personality disorder" described in the *Diagnostic and Statistical Manual of Mental Disorders*, the national standard for psychiatric diagnosis. Town's case provides a clear window into how these personality disorder diagnoses are being used because even a cursory examination of his case casts grave doubt as to whether he fits either criterion.

Town's wife, for one, laughs in disbelief at the idea that her husband was suffering from hearing loss before he headed to Iraq. But since returning, she says, he can't watch TV unless the volume is full-blast, can't use the phone unless its volume is set to high. Medical papers from Fort Carson list Town as having no health problems before serving in Iraq; after, a Fort Carson audiologist documents "functional (non-organic) hearing loss." Town says his right ear, his "good" ear, has lost 50 percent of its hearing; his left is still essentially useless.

He is more disturbed by how his memory has eroded. Since the rocket blast, he has struggled to retain new information. "Like, I'll be driving places, and then I totally forget where I'm going," he says. "Numbers, names, dates—unless I knew them before, I pretty much don't remember." When Town returned to his desk job at Fort Carson, he found himself straining to recall the Army's regulations. "People were like, 'What are you, dumb?' And I'm like, 'No, I'm probably smarter than you. I just can't remember stuff,'" he says, his melancholy suddenly replaced by anger. "They don't understand—I got hit by a rocket."

Untoward Consequences

Those bursts of rage mark the biggest change, says Kristy Town. She says the man she married four years ago was "a real goofball. He'd do funny voices and faces—a great Jim Carrey imitation. When the kids would get a boo-boo, he'd fall on the ground and pretend he got a boo-boo too." Now, she says, "his emotions are all over the place. He'll get so angry at things, and it's not toward anybody. It's toward himself. He blames himself for everything." He has a hard time sleeping and doesn't spend as much time as he used to with the kids. "They get rowdy when they play, and he just has to be alone. It's almost like his nerves can't handle it."

Kristy begins to cry, pauses, before forcing herself to continue. She's been watching him when he's alone, she says. "He kind of . . . zones out, almost like he's in a daze."

In May 2006 Town tried to electrocute himself, dropping his wife's hair dryer into the bathtub. The dryer short-circuited before it could electrify the water. Fort Carson officials put Town in an off-post hospital that specializes in suicidal depression. Town had been promoted to corporal after returning from Iraq; he was stripped of that rank and reduced back to specialist. "When he came back, I tried to be the same," Kristy says. "He just can't. He's definitely not the man he used to be."

Town says his dreams have changed too. They keep taking him back to Ramadi, to the death of a good friend who'd been too near an explosion, taken too much shrapnel to the face. In his dreams Town returns there night after night to soak up the blood.

He stops his description for a rare moment of levity. "Sleep didn't use to be like that," he says. "I used to sleep just fine."

How the Army determined then that Town's behavioral problems existed before his military service is unclear.

Diagnosing the Doctor

How the Army determined then that Town's behavioral problems existed before his military service is unclear. Wexler, the Fort Carson psychologist who made the diagnosis, didn't interview any of Town's family or friends. It's unclear whether he even questioned Town's fellow soldiers in 2-17 Field Artillery, men like Fields, Murray and Michael Forbus, who could have testified to his stability and award-winning performance before the October 2004 rocket attack. As Forbus puts it, before the attack Town was "one of the best in our unit"; after, "the son of a gun was deaf in one ear. He seemed lost and disoriented. It just took the life out of him."

Town finds his diagnosis especially strange because the *Diagnostic Manual* appears to preclude cases like his. It says that a pattern of erratic behavior cannot be labeled a "personality disorder" if it's from a head injury. The specialist asserts that his hearing loss, headaches and anger all began with the rocket attack that knocked him unconscious.

Wexler did not reply to repeated requests seeking comment on Town's diagnosis. But Col. Knorr of Fort Carson's Evans hospital says he's confident his doctors are properly diagnosing personality disorder. The colonel says there is a simple explanation as to why in so many cases the lifelong condition of personality disorder isn't apparent until after serving in Iraq. Traumatic experiences, Knorr says, can trigger a condition that has lain dormant for years. "They may have done fine in high school and before, but it comes out during the stress of service."

"I've never heard of that occurring," says Keith Armstrong, a clinical professor with the Department of Psychiatry at the University of California, San Francisco. Armstrong has been counseling traumatized veterans for more than twenty years at the San Francisco VA; most recently he is the co-author of *Courage After Fire: Coping Strategies for Troops Returning from Iraq and Afghanistan and Their Families.* "Personality disorder is a diagnosis I'm very cautious about," he says. "My question would be, has PTSD been ruled out? It seems to me that if it walks like a duck, looks like a duck, let's see if it's a duck before other factors are implicated."

A half-dozen soldiers from bases across the country who were diagnosed with personality disorder . . . rejected that diagnosis. Most said military doctors tried to force the diagnosis upon them.

Mitigating Factors

Knorr admits that in most cases, before making a diagnosis, his doctors only interview the soldier. But he adds that interviewing family members, untrained to recognize signs of personality disorder, would be of limited value. "The soldier's perception and their parents' perception is that they were fine. But maybe they didn't or weren't able to see that wasn't the case."

Armstrong takes a very different approach. He says family is a "crucial part" of the diagnosis and treatment of soldiers returning from war. The professor sees parents and wives as so important, he encourages his soldiers to invite their families into the counseling sessions. "They bring in particular information that can be helpful," he says. "By not taking advantage of their knowledge and support, I think we're doing soldiers a disservice."

Knorr would not discuss the specifics of Town's case. He did note, however, that his department treats thousands of soldiers each year and says within that population, there are bound to be a small fraction of misdiagnosed cases and dissatisfied soldiers. He adds that the soldiers he's seen diagnosed and discharged with personality disorder are "usually quite pleased."

The Army holds soldiers' medical records and contact information strictly confidential. But *The Nation* was able to locate a half-dozen soldiers from bases across the country who were diagnosed with personality disorder. All of them rejected that diagnosis. Most said military doctors tried to force the diagnosis upon them and turned a blind eye to symptoms of PTSD and physical injury.

Disputed Findings

One such veteran, Richard Dykstra, went to the hospital at Fort Stewart, Georgia, complaining of flashbacks, anger and stomach pains. The doctor there diagnosed personality disorder. Dykstra thinks the symptoms actually stem from PTSD and a bilateral hernia he suffered in Iraq. "When I told her my symptoms, she said, 'Oh, it looks like you've been reading up on PTSD.' Then she basically said I was making it all up," he says.

In her report on Dykstra, Col. Ana Parodi, head of Behavioral Health at Fort Stewart's Winn Army Hospital, writes that the soldier gives a clear description of PTSD symptoms but lays them out with such detail, it's "as if he had memorized the criteria." She concludes that Dykstra has personality disorder, not PTSD, though her report also notes that Dykstra has had "no previous psychiatric history" and that she confirmed the validity of his symptoms with the soldier's wife.

Parodi is currently on leave and could not be reached for comment. Speaking for Fort Stewart, Public Affairs Officer Lieut. Col. Randy Martin says that the Army's diagnosis procedures "have been developed over time, and they are accepted as being fair." Martin said he could not address Dykstra's case specifically because his files have been moved to a storage facility in St. Louis.

Fighting Back

William Wooldridge had a similar fight with the army. The specialist was hauling missiles and tank ammunition outside Baghdad when, he says, a man standing at the side of the road grabbed hold of a young girl and pushed her in front of his truck. "The little girl," Wooldridge says, his voice suddenly quiet, "she looked like one of my daughters."

When he returned to Fort Polk, Louisiana, Wooldridge told his doctor that he was now hearing voices and seeing visions, hallucinations of a mangled girl who would ask him why he had killed her. His doctor told him he had personality disorder. "When I heard that, I flew off the handle because I said, 'Hey, that ain't me. Before I went over there, I was a happy-go-lucky kind of guy.'" Wooldridge says his psychologist, Capt. Patrick Brady of Baynes-Jones Army Community Hospital, saw him for thirty minutes before making his diagnosis. Soon after, Wooldridge was discharged from Fort Polk under Chapter 5–13.

He began to fight that discharge immediately, without success. Then in March 2005, eighteen months after Wooldridge's dismissal, his psychiatrist at the Memphis VA filed papers rejecting Brady's diagnosis and asserting that Wooldridge suffered from PTSD so severe, it made him "totally disabled." Weeks later the Army Discharge Review Board voided

Wooldridge's 5–13 dismissal, but the eighteen months he'd spent lingering without benefits had already taken its toll.

"They put me out on the street to rot, and if I had left things like they were, there would have been no way I could have survived. I would have had to take myself out or had someone do it for me," he says. The way they use personality disorder to diagnose and discharge, he says, "it's like a mental rape. That's the only way I can describe it."

The Military Responds

Captain Brady has since left Fort Polk and is now on staff at Fort Wainwright, Alaska; recently he deployed to Iraq and was unavailable for comment. In a statement, Maj. Byron Strother, chief of the Department of Behavioral Health at Baynes-Jones hospital, writes that allegations that soldiers at Fort Polk are being misdiagnosed "are not true." Strother says diagnoses at his hospital are made "only after careful consideration of all relevant clinical observation, direct examination [and] appropriate testing."

If there are dissatisfied soldiers, says Knorr, the Fort Carson official, "I'll bet not a single one of them has been diagnosed with conditions that are clear-cut and makes them medically unfit, like schizophrenia."

Linda Mosier disputes that. When her son Chris left for Iraq in 2004, he was a "normal kid," she says, who'd call her long-distance and joke about the strange food and expensive taxis overseas. When he returned home for Christmas 2005, "he wouldn't sit down for a meal with us. He just kept walking around. I took him to the department store for slacks, and he was inside rushing around saying, 'Let's go, let's go, let's go.' He wouldn't sleep, and the one time he did, he woke up screaming."

Mosier told his mother of a breaking point in Iraq: a roadside bomb that blew up the truck in front of his. "He said his buddies were screaming. They were on fire," she says, her voice trailing off. "He was there at the end to pick up the hands and arms." After that Mosier started having delusions. Dr. Wexler of Fort Carson diagnosed personality disorder. Soon after, Mosier was discharged under Chapter 5–13.

Mosier returned home, still plagued by visions. In October he put a note on the front door of their Des Moines, Iowa, home saying the Iraqis were after him and he had to protect the family, then shot himself.

Mosier's mother is furious that doctors at Fort Carson treated her son for such a brief period of time and that Wexler, citing confidentiality, refused to tell her anything about that treatment or give her family any direction on how to help Chris upon his return home. She does not believe her son had a personality disorder. "They take a normal kid, he comes back messed up, then nobody was there for him when he came back," Linda says. "They discharged him so they didn't have to treat him."

Wexler did not reply to a written request seeking comment on Mosier's case.

Unlike doctors in the private sector, Army doctors who give questionable diagnoses face no danger of malpractice suits.

The Doctors' Rationale

Today Jon Town is home, in small-town Findlay, Ohio, with no job, no prospects and plenty of time to reflect on how he got there. Diagnosing him with personality disorder may have saved the Army thousands of dollars, he says, but what did Wexler have to gain?

Quite a lot, says Steve Robinson, director of veterans affairs at Veterans for America, a Washington, DC–based soldiers' rights group. Since the Iraq War began, he says, doctors have been facing an overflow of wounded soldiers and a shortage of rooms, supplies and time to treat them. By calling PTSD a personality disorder, they usher one soldier out quickly, freeing up space for the three or four who are waiting.

Terry, the veterans' advocate from IWVO, notes that unlike doctors in the private sector, Army doctors who give questionable diagnoses face no danger of malpractice suits due to *Feres v. U.S.*, a 1950 Supreme Court ruling that bars soldiers from suing for negligence. To maintain that protection, Terry says, most doctors will diagnose personality disorder when prodded to do so by military officials.

That's precisely how the system works, says one military official familiar with the discharge process. The official, who requested anonymity, is a lawyer with Trial Defense Services (TDS), a unit of the Army that guides soldiers through their 5–13 discharge. "Commanders want to get these guys out the door and get it done fast. Even if the next soldier isn't as good, at least he's good to go. He's deployable. So they're telling the docs what diagnosis to give to get what discharge."

The lawyer says he knows this is happening because commanders have told him that they're doing it. "Some have come to me and talked about doing this. They're saying, 'Give me a specific diagnosis. It'll support a certain chapter.'"

Colonel Martin of Fort Stewart said the prospect of commanders pressuring doctors to diagnose personality disorder is "highly unlikely." "Doctors are making these determinations themselves," Martin says. In a statement, Col. William Statz, commander at Fort Polk's Baynes-Jones hospital, says, "Any allegations that clinical decisions are influenced by either political considerations or command pressures, at any level, are untrue."

But a second TDS lawyer, who also demanded anonymity, says he's watched the same process play out at his base. "What I've noticed is right before a unit deploys, we see a spike in 5–13's, as if the commanders are trying to clean house, get rid of the soldiers they don't really need," he says. "The chain of command just wants to eliminate them and get a new body in there fast to plug up the holes." If anyone shows even moderate signs of psychological distress, he says, "they're kicking them to the curb instead of treating them."

Both lawyers say that once a commander steps in and pushes for a 5–13, the diagnosis and discharge are carved in stone fairly fast. After that happens, one lawyer says he points soldiers toward the Army Board for Correction of Military Records, where a 5–13 label could be overturned, and failing that, advises them to seek redress from their representative in Congress. Town did that, contacting Republican Representative Michael Oxley of Ohio, with little success. Oxley, who has since retired, did not return calls seeking comment.

Difficult Appeals

Few cases are challenged successfully or overturned later, say the TDS lawyers. The system, says one, is essentially broken. "Right now, the Army is eating its own. What I want to see is these soldiers getting the right diagnosis, so they can get the right help, not be thrown to the wolves right away. That is what they're doing."

Still, Town tries to remain undaunted. He got his story to Robinson of Veterans for America, who brought papers on his case to an October meeting with several top Washington officials, including Deputy Surgeon General Gale Pollock, Assistant Surgeon General Bernard DeKoning and Republican Senator Kit Bond of Missouri. There Robinson laid out the larger 5–13 problem and submitted a briefing specifically on Town.

"We got a very positive response," Robinson says. "After we presented, they were almost appalled, like we are every day. They said, 'We didn't know this was happening.'" Robinson says the deputy surgeon general promised to look into Town's case and the others presented to her. Senator Bond, whose son has served in Iraq, floated the idea of a Congressional hearing if the 5–13 issue isn't resolved. The senator did not return calls seeking comment.

In the meantime, Town is doing his best to keep his head in check. He says his nightmares have been waning in recent weeks, but most of his problems persist. He's thinking of going to a veterans support group in Toledo, forty-five miles north of Findlay. There will be guys there who have been through this, he says, vets who understand.

Town hesitates, his voice suddenly much softer. "I have my good days and my bad days," he says. "It all depends on whether I wake up in Findlay or Iraq."

12

Military Doctors Provide Veterans with Quality Mental Health Care

Antonette Zeiss

Antonette Zeiss is the deputy chief consultant for the Office of Mental Health Services, U.S. Department of Veterans Affairs.

The U.S. Department of Veterans Affairs (VA) understands that events and conditions experienced by returning veterans may result in both physical and emotional or mental injury. The goal of the VA is to treat veterans as whole patients and address all issues, both physical and mental. To that end, the VA has implemented a number of new initiatives and programs to not only increase its capacity, but also to enhance the quality and continuity of care. The VA remains committed and prepared to address the continued needs of veterans by providing the highest quality of care possible.

I am pleased to ... discuss the ongoing steps that the Department of Veterans Affairs (VA) is taking in order to meet the mental health care needs of our Nation's veterans. ... I would like to take this opportunity to describe a general overview of the mental health services provided by VA. VA has devoted resources to develop appropriate programs, and closely follow emerging evidence to refine our understanding and program development for these returning veterans.

VA provides mental health services to veterans in all our medical facility patient care settings. I will provide an over-

Antonette Zeiss, "Military Mental Health Treatment," Statement before the U.S. House of Representatives Committee on Oversight and Government Reform, May 24, 2007.

view of all these services, since returning veterans will need this full array of VA services, and I will focus more specifically on some newly developed programs for our returning veterans.

Our goal is to treat a veteran as a whole patient—to treat a patient's physical illnesses as well as any mental disorders he or she may be facing.

Mental health services are provided in specialty mental health settings in all medical facilities, including inpatient, outpatient, and substance abuse care. VA also provides services for homeless veterans, including transitional housing paired with services to address the social, vocational, and mental health problems that contributed to becoming homeless. In addition, mental health care is being integrated into primary care clinics, community-based outpatient clinics [CBOCs], VA nursing homes, and residential care facilities. Veterans with PTSD [post traumatic stress disorder] are served by mental health professionals with specialized expertise in all medical facilities, and VA has inpatient and residential rehabilitation options across the country. Veterans with a serious mental illness are seen in specialized programs, such as mental health intensive case management, psychosocial rehabilitation and recovery day programs and work programs. VA employs full- and part-time psychiatrists and full- and part-time psychologists who work in collaboration with social workers, mental health nurses, counselors, rehabilitation specialists, and other clinicians to provide a full continuum of mental health services for veterans. The numbers of these mental health professionals have been growing steadily as a result of focused efforts to build mental health staff and programs. Appropriate attention to the physical and mental health needs of veterans will have a positive impact on their successful re-integration into the U.S. economy and society as a whole. Accurate VA projections for staffing needs and funding costs will ensure ready access to adequate and timely mental health and social services.

We have seen that many returning veterans have injuries of the mind and spirit as well as the body. For veterans of prior eras, we have learned that mental disorders can increase the risk for certain physical illnesses, and vice versa. In addition, current returning veterans experience events that result in both physical and emotional injuries. Our goal is to treat a veteran as a whole patient—to treat a patient's physical illnesses as well as any mental disorders he or she may be facing.

Visible in Communities

In addition to the care described in medical facilities and their related CBOCs, VA's Vet Centers provide counseling and readjustment services to returning war veterans. It is now well established that rehabilitation for war-related PTSD and other military-related readjustment problems, along with the treatment of the physical wounds of war, is central to VA's continuum of health care programs specific to the needs of veterans. The Vet Center service mission goes beyond medical care in providing a holistic mix of services designed to treat the veteran as a whole person in his/her community setting. Vet Centers provide an alternative to traditional access for mental health care some veterans may be reluctant to access in our medical centers and clinics. Vet Centers are staffed by interdisciplinary teams that include psychologists, nurses and social workers.

VA will be expanding the number of Vet Centers from 209 to 232 [from 2007 to 2009]. Some Vet Centers have established telehealth linkages with VA medical centers that extend VA mental health service delivery to remote areas to underserved veteran populations, including Native Americans on reservations at some sites. Vet Centers also offer telehealth services to expand the reach to an even broader audience. Vet Centers address the psychological and social readjustment and rehabilitation process for veterans and support ongoing enhancements under the VA Mental Health Strategic Plan.

Vet Centers provided readjustment counseling services to over 228,000 all-era combat veterans in Fiscal Year [FY] 2006 and, of these, over 127,000 veterans were provided substantial face-to-face counseling services, and over 101,000 veterans were seen on outreach. The Vet Centers provided over one million visits to veterans in Fiscal Year 2006.

The Vet Center strategy is to intervene early to facilitate a successful post-war readjustment in a safe and confidential setting.

The Vet Center program addresses the veteran's full range of needs within the family and community. The service functions provided to veterans by the Vet Center program are as follows:

- Community-based service units emphasizing post-war rehabilitation in an informal setting;

- Extensive community outreach activities;

- A varied mix of direct counseling and supportive social services addressing the holistic psycho-social needs of veterans in their post-war readjustment;

- Assessment for war-related readjustment problems to include PTSD in all cases;

- Assessment and treatment of military related sexual trauma; and

- Family counseling when needed for the readjustment of the veteran.

Since 2003, the Vet Centers also provide bereavement services to surviving family members of service men and women killed while serving on active duty. The Vet Center strategy is to intervene early to facilitate a successful post-war readjustment in a safe and confidential setting. The bereavement program has seen over 1,200 family members of over 900 fallen warriors most of whom were killed in action in Operation Enduring Freedom [the war in Afghanistan begun in 2002]/ Operation Iraqi Freedom [the war in Iraq begun in 2003] (OEF/OIF).

Combat Stress

Care for OEF/OIF veterans is among the highest priorities in VA's mental health care system. For these veterans, VA has the opportunity to apply what has been learned through research and clinical experience about the diagnosis and treatment of mental health conditions to intervene early; and to work to prevent the chronic or persistent courses of illnesses that have occurred in veterans of prior eras.

In response to the growing numbers of veterans returning from combat in OEF/OIF, the Vet Centers initiated an aggressive outreach campaign to welcome home and educate returning service members at military demobilization and National Guard and Reserve sites. Through its community outreach and brokering efforts, the Vet Center program also provides many veterans the means of access to other Veterans Health Administration (VHA) and Veterans Benefits Administration (VBA) programs. To augment this effort, the Vet Center program recruited and hired 100 OEF/OIF veterans to provide the bulk of this outreach to their fellow veterans.

Medical facility programs also have been established to do "inreach" to OEF/OIF veterans and provide education, support, and mental health specialty services when needed. These programs are established in most facilities, beginning with sites that had the highest rates of returning veterans, and continue to be expanded each year. In addition, we have placed mental health specialists in all four of the initial national Polytrauma Centers and now in the 21 VISN [Veterans Integrated Service Network] Polytrauma programs. We recently funded a Transitional Housing program for veterans who have needed polytrauma care, with mental health staff fully represented. Throughout VHA, there is a sense of urgency about reaching out to OEF/OIF veterans, engaging them in care, screening them for mental health conditions, and making diagnoses when appropriate.

Since the start of OEF/OIF through the end of the first quarter of FY 2007, 686,306 service members have been discharged and become eligible for VA care. Of those, 229,015 (33 percent) have sought VA care. Of those that have sought care (33 percent), mental health problems are the second most common, with 37 percent (83,889) reporting concerns that lead to a mental health diagnosis or indicate that one is possible and should be further evaluated.

Growing Mental Health Needs

While VA must be attentive to PTSD, we also must ensure that evaluation is comprehensive and attentive to mental health problems generally, so that we can provide the best evaluation, diagnosis, and treatment for returning veterans. Of those reporting a possible mental health concern, Post Traumatic Stress Disorder (PTSD) was most frequently implicated (39,243), with Nondependent Abuse of Drugs (33,099), and Depressive Disorders (27,023) the next most commonly suggested problems.

In addition, VA is aware that the proportion of new veterans seeking VA care who are identified as having a possible mental health problem has climbed over the years. For example, the proportion with mental health concerns in the report at the end of FY 2005 was 31 percent, compared to 37 percent in the most recent report. There are many possible explanations of this finding including: extended deployments, more difficult circumstances, and positive impact of efforts to destigmatize the seeking of mental health services. Regardless of the causes, VA is aware that there is an increasing demand for mental health-related services. VA is prepared to devote increasing resources to serving these growing mental health needs. The utilization pattern for war veterans from other eras indicates that these veterans will require sustained services and will increase in numbers over time.

Since the beginning of hostilities in Afghanistan and Iraq, the Vet Centers have seen over 165,000 OEF/OIF veterans, of which almost 116,000 were outreach contacts seen primarily in group settings at military demobilization and National Guard and Reserve sites. A similar outreach program conducted during the first Gulf War received the commendation of the President's Advisory Committee on Gulf War Veterans' Illnesses.

Strategic Planning

VHA completed its Comprehensive Mental Health Strategic Plan (MHSP) in 2004 and began implementation in spring 2005. Our strategic plan reinforces that mental health is an important part of veterans' overall health. VA is committed to eliminating barriers separating mental health from the rest of health care. The plan also recognizes the needs of our returning OEF/OIF veterans.

The Mental Health Initiative was established to provide funding to support the implementation of the MHSP outside of the Veterans Equitable Resource Allocation (VERA) model. To assist in planning the funding for the Mental Health Initiative, the MHSP was divided into four key areas—(1) enhancing capacity and access for mental health services; (2) integrating mental health and primary care; (3) transforming mental health specialty care to emphasize recovery and rehabilitation; and (4) implementation of evidence-based care.

There are multiple funded programs in each of these areas. We have improved capacity and access in numerous ways, supporting hiring of new mental health professionals throughout the system. Moreover, we have expanded mental health services in Community Based Outreach Clinics either with on-site staffing or by telemental health, thus providing care closer to the homes of veterans in rural areas. We also have enhanced both PTSD and substance abuse specialty care services, and programs that recognize the common co-occurrence of these problems. We are fostering the integration of mental health and primary care by funding evidence-based programs in over 80 sites, with more [in the] planning stages, as well as through the already-mentioned placement of mental health staff in CBOCs. In addition, we are extending this principle to the care of home-bound veterans by funding mental health positions in Home Based Primary Care. This program has traditionally served older veterans, but current needs show that it also will serve some seriously wounded OEF/OIF veterans. It can allow veterans to live at home, with their families, as an alternative to institutional long-term care, when injuries are profound and sustained rehabilitation and other care is needed. The mental health professionals who will work with these teams also can support the family caregivers, who provide heroic care for injured veterans.

Screening veterans . . . is a vital first step towards helping veterans become resilient and recover from the psychological wounds of war.

VA will be working to emphasize recovery and rehabilitation in specialty mental health services by funding additional psychosocial rehabilitation programs, expanding residential rehabilitation services, increasing the number of beds and the degree of coordination in homeless programs, extending Mental Health Intensive Case Management, and funding a recovery coordinator in each medical center.

Post Traumatic Stress Disorder

VA's approach to PTSD is to promote early recognition of this condition for those who meet formal criteria for diagnosis and those with partial symptoms. The goal is to make evidence-based treatments available early to prevent chronicity and lasting impairment. Screening veterans for PTSD is a vital first step towards helping veterans become resilient and recover from the psychological wounds of war. Veterans are screened on a routine basis through contact in Primary Care Clinics. In instances when there is a positive screen, patients are further evaluated and referred to a mental health provider for further follow-up, as necessary.

If a veteran first enters the system through a clinical program other than primary care, screening for PTSD will be done in that setting. In addition, screening occurs for depression, substance abuse, and military sexual trauma. Recently, screening for Traumatic Brain Injury (TBI) became a standard component of VA's screening. While TBI is not a mental health problem, it has many intersections with mental health problems and its recognition is an essential component of holistic care.

Screening is only valuable if the system is set up to note positive screens and conduct timely follow-up of them. When the follow-up reveals there is a likely diagnosis, or early signs that a veteran is having increasing mental health problems, timely treatment for those problems is necessary. VA has the capacity to provide screening, evaluation of positive screens, and appropriate treatment. As we continue to implement the Mental Health Strategic Plan, which has guided the efforts described, and continue to benefit from the funding available in the Mental Health Enhancement Initiative, our capacity will continue to grow, to enable us to continue serving a growing number of returning veterans.

In providing follow-up, we have outpatient and inpatient programs available (a total of over 220 programs and more in development). We have extensive training efforts in a variety of different approaches including Cognitive Processing Therapy and Prolonged Exposure Therapy. We are partnering with the Department of Defense (DoD) to make these training opportunities available to DoD mental health staff.

Medications can be an effective component of care for PTSD, but have not been shown to have the same level of effectiveness in both alleviating symptoms and restoring function and performance. Our integrated care system allows coordination of effective psychotherapy with needed medication supports.

Sometimes mild to moderate PTSD symptoms, without a full diagnosis, represent normal reactions to highly abnormal situations. Many returning veterans will recover without treatment, with support from their families, communities, and employers. In fact, what is most striking about our service members and veterans is not their vulnerability, but their resilience. When people prefer treatment, we encourage it. When they are reluctant, we watch them over time, and urge treatment if symptoms persist or worsen.

We acknowledge the need to reevaluate and improve the mental health care and services provided to our Nation's veterans, and we are committed to ensuring that VA provides the highest quality of care possible.

Suicide Watch

Suicide prevention is a major priority for VA and we are on the watch for suicide among our veterans. Research about suicides among OEF/OIF returnees is currently under way to teach us more about how to address the issues surrounding this tragic event.

VA also set aside our first Suicide Prevention Awareness Day, which fell on March 1, 2007. We plan on this becoming an annual event. During our first Suicide Prevention Awareness Day, VA staff members who come in contact with patients received training on how to assess and respond to crisis situations. Our goal is to make the point that in VA, suicide prevention is everyone's business—not just that of our mental health providers—everyone who comes into contact with our veterans and their families plays an important role.

The mental health needs of our veterans are as important as their physical needs. We acknowledge the need to reevaluate and improve the mental health care and services provided to our Nation's veterans, and we are committed to ensuring that VA provides the highest quality of care possible.

13

Veterans' Access to Quality Health Care Is Often Limited

George Ondick

George Ondick is executive director of the AmVets (American Veterans), Department of Ohio.

Research has shown that veterans living in rural settings are generally in poorer health than their urban counterparts, and they often experience problems in accessing veterans health care facilities. Outreach programs were beneficial to veterans in rural areas, but they were shut down due to budget constraints. It is logical to locate veterans health care facilities where they can provide services to the largest number of veterans, but those living in remote areas are just as deserving of medical benefits as those in densely populated areas. The outreach programs should be reinstated, and several other programs should be improved and have their budgets increased.

In a 2004 study of more than 767,000 veterans by Veterans Affairs researchers shows those in rural areas are in poorer health than their urban counterparts. The findings, reported in the October [2006]*American Journal of Public Health*, validate recent and ongoing VA efforts to expand health care for rural patients.

"We need to think about veterans who live in rural settings as a special population, and we need to carefully consider their needs when designing healthcare delivery systems,"

George Ondick, "Veterans' Issues in Appalachia," Statement before the Combined House-Senate Committee on Veterans' Affairs on Remote and Rural Veteran Issues, May 29, 2007. Reproduced by permission of the author.

said study leader William B. Weeks, MD, MBA, a physician and researcher with the White River Junction [Vermont] VA Medical Center [VAMC] and Dartmounth Medical School. Senior author on the study was Jonathan B. Perlin, MD, PhD, VA's acting under secretary for health.

The study included 767,109 veterans who had used VA healthcare between 1996 and 1999. VA had then just begun setting up Community Based Outpatient Clinics (CBOCs) to provide primary care closer to home for rural veterans. Today there are nearly 700 CBOCs in VA's nationwide system, and recent recommendations from VA's Capital Asset Realignment for Enhanced Service (CARES) initiative call for the establishment of more than 150 additional CBOCs.

Indefensible Inequities

Many veterans living in remote areas have found several problems on reaching the VA Medical Centers and VA Clinics; some, due to their inability to obtain transportation, and others due to inability to pay for their transportation. In Ohio, most County Veterans Service Commissions will provide transportation for "qualified" veterans. However, a disabled veteran going for VA Healthcare, may receive from the VA mileage of 11c [cents] per mile with a $3 deductible each way. Compare that 11c to a VA employee receiving 48.5c which is considerably more for the same trip and no deductible. Why is there a difference? The Veteran has to pay the same $3.50 for fuel as does the VA employee.

Veterans Affairs Community Based Outpatient Clinics (VA CBOC's or CBOC) were established to change from the centralized idea of admitting many veterans to a hospital for treatment, to smaller, more localized service on an outpatient basis. This seemingly is much better for the patient, the family and the VA budget. It had worked quite well until the veterans' healthcare outreach was stopped due to budget restrictions.

The VA Health Administration had an outreach program that worked quite well. The VAMCs would send a team (a doctor, nurse, technician and admin clerk) to various remote areas to do the routine healthcare. In southern Ohio, there were many examples: a team went to Pomeroy, 88 miles away from the Chillicothe VAMC, and Jackson, 45 miles away from the Chillicothe VAMC, as well as several other locations. In Jackson, they set up shop in a VSO [veterans service organization] post. In Pomeroy, they used part of the Holzer Clinic. There were many "outreach clinics" in operation, until the budget problems in January 2003 caused their closing.

Those veterans who depended on outreach visits must now travel 80 or more miles to visit a doctor to get their treatments.

An Undue Burden

The VA policy on establishing VA CBOCs was established so a veteran would not have to travel over 35 miles to obtain healthcare. It was changed to 40 miles. Now the strange thing is in northern Ohio, there are VA Clinics fairly well covering all geographic areas and only one facility is scheduled to close and it is within 40 miles of VA clinics on each side. This gives us an idea of the problem. In the western portion, the Cincinnati area, there are plenty of VA facilities, many within 30 miles of one another. In remote/rural southeast Ohio, it is a different story. The CBOC program has been curtailed. There are VA CBOCs in Athens, Portsmouth and Marietta, which cover as much area as 20 facilities in other areas of Ohio. Those veterans who depended on outreach visits must now travel 80 or more miles to visit a doctor to get their treatments and then drive back 80 or so miles. For those needing radiation, they are further transferred to Cincinnati in a van. In Cincinnati, they are given their radiation treatment, which causes great nausea, then delivered back to their vehicle for the 80 miles or more drive home. What a way to say thank you for your service to our great nation!!!

[Rural] veterans served and sacrificed just as much as their counterparts in large populated areas.

The understandable rationale is that VA facilities are set up in areas that will service the largest number of veterans and thus being cost effective. This put us in our present co-nundrum of providing for veterans in remote/rural areas. Those veterans served and sacrificed just as much as their counterparts in large populated areas. It is AMVETS' position that we need the VA medical outreach reestablished for those in remote/rural areas of Ohio and the Nation. We owe our rural area veterans this service and more.

The AMVETS is currently providing outreach to veterans in southern Ohio, filing claims on their behalf. With each claim we file, we create another access dilemma for the veterans we serve. Again, it is AMVETS' position that we need the VA medical outreach reestablished for those in remote/rural areas of Ohio and the Nation. I also believe [that since] the VA created an Office of Rural Health Care it should be funded, and supported.

Recent history demonstrates why Congress should pass legislation to make VA health care funding mandatory spending.

Legislative Priorities

I would also like to take the time to reiterate the AMVETS legislative priorities for 2007; they are as follows:

The Department of Veterans Affairs (VA) Fiscal Year 2008 Budget—The President's budget request for VA in Fiscal Year (FY) 2008 seeks approximately $86.7 billion for veterans' benefits and services. This amounts to $39.4 billion in discretionary funding and $44.9 billion in mandatory appropriations. In FY 2008, AMVETS requests roughly $43.6 billion in discretionary funding.

Mandatory Funding for VA Health Care—In May 2001, President George W. Bush signed Executive Order 13214 creating the President's Task Force to Improve Health Care Delivery for Our Nation's Veterans (PTF). In May 2003, the PTF issued its final report and recommended that the Federal Government should provide full funding ... and that full funding should occur through modifications to the current budget and appropriations process, by using a mandatory funding mechanism. Recent history demonstrates why Congress should pass legislation to make VA health care funding mandatory spending. In FY 2005, VA faced a $1.3 billion shortfall in spending and Congress had to include additional funding in emergency appropriations. For FY 2007, Congress failed to pass the annual VA spending bill and the department is operating under a Continuing Resolution well below FY 2007 requested levels.

Extend Enrollment for OEF [Operation Enduring Freedom. The war in Afghanistan begun in 2002]/OIF [Operation Iraqi Freedom, the war in Iraq begun in 2003] Veterans—H.R. 612 and S. 383 introduced in the House of Representatives and the Senate, respectively, would extend from two years to five years, following discharge or release from active duty, the eligibility period for veterans who served in combat during or after the Persian Gulf War. Continued eligibility would allow veterans to receive hospital care, medical services, or nursing home care provided by the Secretary of Veterans Affairs, notwithstanding a lack of evidence to conclude that their condition is attributable to such service. AMVETS fully supports the passage of legislation to extend the two-year priority enrollment for OEF/OIF veterans.

Seamless Transition—In March 2007, GAO [Government Accountability Office] testified that the Department of Defense (DOD) and VA were still having problems sharing the necessary medical records the VA needed to determine whether service members' medical conditions allowed participation in VA's rehabilitation activities. Congress should require the two agencies to develop electronic medical records that are interoperable, bi-directional, and standards-based. Congress should also require DOD to conduct mandatory separation physicals for all separating service personnel and also utilize the Benefits Delivery at Discharge (BDD) joint separation exam that was developed and agreed to by both agencies.

Increasing Funding

Post Traumatic Stress Disorder (PTSD) and Traumatic Brain Injury (TBI)—VA operates a network of more than 190 specialized Post Traumatic Stress Disorder (PTSD) outpatient treatment programs throughout the country. Vet Centers are seeing a rapid increase in their enrollment. Equally important, AMVETS is concerned about the lack of awareness and screening among health care professionals for Traumatic Brain Injury (TBI). PTSD and TBI clinically present the same symptoms and the problem for medical personnel is trying to differentiate between PTSD and TBI. VA's approach to PTSD is to promote early recognition of this condition and the same must be done for TBI. In addition, there is no medical diagnostic code specific to TBI. AMVETS is asking Congress to increase funding for PTSD and TBI, with an emphasis on developing improved screening techniques and assigning a new medical code specifically for TBI.

VA Burial Allowance—VA reimbursement benefits were first instituted in 1973 and provided $150 in reimbursements for deaths that were not service-related. In 2001 the plot allowance was increased for the first time in more than 28 years, to $300. The non-service-connected burial allowance was last adjusted in 1978 and now also provides $300. AMVETS supports increasing the non-service-connected burial benefit from $300 to $1,270 and increasing the plot allowance from $300 to $745, an amount proportionally equal to the original benefit. In 2001, Congress increased the burial allowance for service-related deaths from $500 to $2,000. Prior to this adjustment, the allowance had been untouched since 1988. AMVETS recommends increasing the service-related burial benefit from $2,000 to $4,100, restoring the value of burial costs to its original proportionate level.

VA Claims Backlog—The VA Claims Backlog is now over 600,000 outstanding claims and it continues to grow at a rapid rate. VA estimates that over 263,000 OEF/OIF veterans will seek VA services and most will want to file a claim. At the end of fiscal year 2006, rating-related compensation claims were pending an average of 127 days, which is 16 days more than at the end of fiscal year 2003. During the same period, the inventory of rating-related claims grew by almost half, in part because of increased filing of claims, including those filed by veterans of the Iraq and Afghanistan conflicts. Meanwhile, appeals resolution remains a lengthy process, taking an average of 657 days in fiscal year 2006. Overall, a lack of quality control is central to this issue and VA must establish a long-term strategy focused on attaining quality and not merely achieving quotas in claims processing. AMVETS supports increased funding for VA to hire more Full Time Equivalents (FTEs) in order to address the backlog. AMVETS also supports the practice of putting adjudication officers in VA offices aboard active duty military bases.

14

Veterans Should Receive Compensated Private Health Care

Michael F. Cannon

Michael F. Cannon is the director of health policy studies at the Cato Institute. He is also coauthor of Healthy Competition: What's Holding Back Health Care and How to Free It.

Most people agree that America's veterans should receive top-notch medical care and benefits. But the reality of that ideal is compromised by bureaucratic problems, scandals, and funding shortages. The Veterans Health Administration (VHA) could avoid many of these problems if the federal government gave a pay raise to all military members and veterans and allowed them to purchase their own private insurance to cover service-related injuries and illnesses. Such an initiative would put the money and the health care choices directly into the hands of the veterans. Moreover, such a move would make Congress and the American public much more aware of the true costs of foreign policy decisions.

The scandal unfolding at Walter Reed Army Medical Center and the Veterans Health Administration (VHA) [over slumlike conditions] has me wondering: could we improve veterans' health benefits by eliminating the VHA?

[In March 2007,] *Newsweek* reported the stories of Jeffrey Lucey and Jonathan Shulze, two Iraq war veterans who recently took their own lives after having difficulty obtaining mental health services from the VHA.

The VHA is supposed to provide medical, mental health, and rehabilitative care to former members of the armed services. Yet it presents many of the same symptoms of other government-run health care systems, such as the Defense Health Program, which operates Walter Reed.

At the VHA, *Newsweek* found "a grim portrait of an overloaded bureaucracy cluttered with red rape; veterans having to wait weeks or months for mental-health care and other appointments; [and] families sliding into debt as VA case managers study disability claims over many months." Other symptoms include rapidly growing outlays, political games over funding levels, and a lack of accountability.

A Better Way

Everyone—right, left, libertarian—wants our vets to be well cared for. But is a government-run system the best way to do it? Or might there be ways to provide vets better health care?

In essence, the VHA combines health and disability insurance with medical care delivery. Taxpayers bear the financial risk of veterans needing care for service-related injuries. When those injuries happen, the taxpayers cover the cost of care and the federal government delivers the care through government-owned VA hospitals.

Consider an alternative. Suppose that instead of providing those benefits itself, the federal government increased military pay enough to enable new personnel to purchase private insurance to cover service-related injuries and illnesses. (Those include illnesses that manifest themselves years later, such as mental illnesses or birth defects that result from exposure to hazardous substances.)

Making It Work

The pay raise would have to be enough to allow new personnel to purchase "veterans' insurance" that is at least as good as they would receive through the VHA. When they enlist or accept a commission, personnel could be required to purchase health and disability insurance that covers any service-related injuries or illness during that enlistment or commission.

Private insurers would calibrate premium according to the risks posed by different jobs. Premiums would be higher for helicopter pilots and lower for desk jockeys. To enable everyone to purchase coverage, Congress would have to increase pay for each position according to the risk it entails, much [as] it increases pay during combat. That would basically front-load the cost of caring for service-related injuries.

Vets who would have used the VHA would instead use their private insurance to purchase care from private facilities—not government facilities.

Vets who would have used the VHA would instead use their private insurance to purchase care from private facilities—not government facilities.

The Advantages

Privatizing both the insurance and delivery components of veterans' health benefits could have a number of benefits.

First, it would let veterans control the money. That means the system would serve *them*, not the politicians or the bureaucracy.

Second, it would allow vets to choose where they receive medical care and could reduce waiting times for care. Would the scandalous neglect and mistreatment of patients at Walter Reed have occurred if those same vets had the choice to go elsewhere? Patrick Feges of Sugar Land, Texas, was injured in Ramadi [Iraq] by a mortar. He waited 17 months for his first disability check from the VHA. A private insurer with that kind of reputation would have a hard time attracting customers.

Third, the premiums that private insurers charge would give new personnel an independent assessment of the risk posed by different military jobs.

Fourth, those risk-based premiums would increase when conflict seems imminent, in effect front-loading those war-related costs. Harvard professor Linda Bilmes estimates that caring for an anticipated 700,000 veterans of Iraq and Afghanistan will cost between $350 billion and $700 billion. Since Congress would have to increase pay enough for military personnel to insure against those costs up front, they would have an additional disincentive to start wars. The officials who make such decisions would have to plan for those costs themselves, rather than pass the buck to their successors.

The Best Role for the VA

Some have argued that the VA should get out of medical care delivery by selling off its hospitals and giving veterans a voucher that they could use to purchase medical care wherever they like. That probably would increase the quality of care that veterans receive. But that would also leave VHA in the health and disability insurance business.

It seems to me that a better approach would be to give vouchers to all personnel currently in the system, but increase pay and let private carriers insure against service-related injuries for all new enlistments and commissions. Such a system could improve the quality of care for vets. It also would give Congress, the armed forces, and the public a lot of very useful information about the costs of foreign policy decisions.

Organizations to Contact

The editors have compiled the following list of organizations concerned with the issues debated in this book. The descriptions are derived from materials provided by the organizations. All have publications or information available for interested readers. The list was compiled on the date of publication of the present volume; the information provided here may change. Be aware that many organizations may take several weeks or longer to respond to inquiries, so allow as much time as possible.

American Legion
PO Box 1055, Indianapolis, IN   46206
(317) 630-1200 • fax: (202) 861-2786
Web site: www.legion.org

The American Legion is the nation's largest veterans' service organization for veterans who served in wartime. Founded in 1919, it now has nearly three million members. Politically active in lobbying for the interests of veterans, particularly in the area of pensions and medical benefits, the organization also fosters broad volunteer activities and commemorative events honoring veterans. It publishes the *American Legion* magazine.

American Veterans (AMVETS)
4647 Forbes Blvd., Lanham, MD   20706-4380
(301) 459-9600
Web site: www.amvets.org

For more than sixty years, the AMVETS organization has continued its objective to assist all veterans, through professional counseling by service officers, legislative lobbying on Capitol Hill, and volunteering at hospitals (both AMVETS members and AMVETS Ladies Auxiliary). There is also strong support and involvement in community service and initiative to improve the lives of local veterans. AMVETS publishes the *American Veteran* magazine and has a membership of approximately 180,000, organized through local posts.

Coalition to Salute America's Heroes

100 Broadway, Ossining, NY   10562
(914) 432-5400 • fax: (914) 923-3898
Web site: www.saluteheroes.org

Founded in 2004, the Coalition to Salute America's Heroes is dedicated to easing the trauma and transition of wounded soldiers and their families through the difficult recovery period following combat-related injuries. It has been awarded the coveted "Best in America" seal, granted to those charitable organizations that meet criteria for public accountability, program effectiveness, and cost effectiveness (96 percent of contributions goes directly to service members and their families). It sponsors an annual Road to Recovery conference to unite wounded veterans and their families across the nation and share and support each other through the recovery process.

Disabled American Veterans (DAV)

3725 Alexandria Pike, Cold Spring, KY   41076
(859) 441-7300
Web site: www.dav.org

The Disabled American Veterans have more than 1.2 million members working to build better lives for disabled veterans and their families. The organization offers free assistance for obtaining benefits and services. Its largest endeavor is the National Service Program, operating through eighty-eight offices nationwide, that directly represents veterans with claims for benefits from the Department of Veterans Affairs and the Department of Defense. DAV also operates the National Voluntary Service Program, through which veterans and concerned citizens provide services for their fellow disabled veterans, such as transportation to and from VA medical facilities. DAV is not a government agency and does not accept federal funds; it is fully funded through membership dues and public contributions.

Military Order of the Purple Heart
National Headquarters, Springfield, VA 22151-3915
(703) 642-5360 • fax: (703) 642-1841
Web site: www.purpleheart.org

The Military Order of the Purple Heart is a special organization whose membership is limited to the community of combat-wounded veterans (or civilian nationals so injured). The Purple Heart organization states its mission as one "to foster an environment of good will and camaraderie among combat-wounded veterans, promote patriotism, support necessary legislative initiatives, and, most importantly, provide service to all veterans and their families."

Military Retirees Grass Roots Group (MRGRG)
Web site: http://mrgrg-ms.org

The MRGRG is a coalition of mostly retired military personnel united by common interests in protecting and preserving benefits promised to them by military recruiters and officials in return for their service enlistments. Most of the veterans are from World War II and the Korean War, but more recently retired veterans have joined forces with the group. The group is most known for its efforts in trying to preserve "free lifetime medical care and benefits," which it asserts was promised to most of its members by military recruiters.

National Association for Uniformed Services (NAUS)
5535 Hempstead Way, Springfield, VA 22151
(703) 750-1342 • fax: (703) 354-4380
Web site: www.naus.org

The National Association for Uniformed Services is the only military-affiliated association whose membership is open to all military branches and ranks. It represents and provides assistance in all areas of military service, including recruitment, retention, spousal support, and survivorship. It also lobbies and promotes members' interests in Washington. NAUS publishes the *Uniformed Services Journal.*

National Priorities Project
17 New South St., Northampton, MA   01060
(413) 584-9556 • fax: (413) 586-9647
Web site: www.nationalpriorities.org

The National Priorities Project is a nonprofit research organization that analyzes and clarifies federal data for the general public. The organization focuses on issues involving federal budgets and spending, as well as other key policies affecting government at all levels.

U.S. Department of Veterans Affairs (VA)
Washington, DC
VA Benefits: (800) 827-1000
Web site: www.va.gov

Created expressly by the U.S. Congress to assist all veterans with services and benefits, the VA oversees, among other things, the administration of medical care and general federal benefits to veterans. Its Veterans Health Administration has direct responsibility for the handling of veterans' claims for health benefits, as well as the operation of military medical facilities and health care providers. It estimates that more than 70 million persons are potentially eligible for VA benefits and services as veterans, survivors, or family members.

Veterans for America (VFA)
1025 Vermont Ave. NW, 7th Fl., Washington, DC   20005
(202) 483-9222 • fax: (202) 483-9312
Web site: www.veteransforamerica.org

The Veterans for America, a leading advocacy and humanitarian organization, states its primary mission as "ensuring that our country meets the needs of service members and veterans who have served in Afghanistan in Operation Enduring Freedom (OEF) and in Operation Iraqi Freedom (OIF)." To that end, the VFA specifically focuses on psychological trauma and traumatic brain injuries associated with these military campaigns.

Vietnam Veterans of America (VVA)
8605 Cameron St., Suite 400, Silver Springs, MD 20910
(301) 585-0519
Web site: www.vva.org

This organization, of particular interest to those veterans who served during the Vietnam War (1965–1975), has more than fifty thousand individual members and 630 local chapters. Its stated goals are to promote and support the full range of issues facing veterans of that era. It publishes the *VVA Veteran*, and is primarily responsible for dedicating (in 1978) the Vietnam Veterans Memorial in Washington, D.C., that preserves the names of more than fifty-eight thousand deceased American veterans.

Wounded Warriors
1719 N. Sixtieth St., Omaha, NE 68104
(402) 502-7557 • fax: (402) 502-4872
Web site: www.woundedwarriors.org

Wounded Warriors is dedicated to the welfare, recovery, and psychological and financial support of families of wounded military personnel. It is in the process of building an eighty-acre family retreat in northern Nebraska for the use of families of wounded, injured, or killed soldiers. It also donates the use of two luxury condominiums, in Florida and Texas, for one-week retreats to reunite and strengthen the families of veterans who have undergone the injury or death of their loved ones. Qualified beneficiaries are those soldiers (any branch of the armed forces) who were injured or wounded during combat operations as defined by the Department of Defense. Wounded Warriors is a family-oriented program, and qualifying service members must have dependent children.

Bibliography

Books

Keith Armstrong and Suzanne Best

Courage After Fire. Berkeley, CA: Ulysses, 2006.

Rodney R. Baker and Wade E. Pickren

Psychology and the Department of Veterans Affairs: A Historical Analysis of Training, Research, Practice, and Advocacy. Washington, DC: American Psychological Association Press, 2007.

P.J. Budahn

Veterans' Guide to Benefits, 4th ed. Mechanicsburg, PA: Stackpole, 2005.

Timothy R. Dillingham and Praxedes V. Belandres, eds.

Rehabilitation of the Injured Combatant. Washington, DC: U.S. Army, Borden Institute, Walter Reed Army Medical Center, 1998.

Phillip Longman

Best Care Anywhere: Why VA Health Care Is Better than Yours. Sausalito, CA: Polipoint, 2007.

John D. Roche

Veterans' PTSD Handbook: How to File and Collect on Claims for Post-Traumatic Stress Disorder. Dulles, VA: Potomac, 2007.

John D. Roche

Veterans' Survival Guide, Dulles, VA: Potomac, 2006.

Wilbur J. Scott

Vietnam Veterans Since the War: The Politics of PTSD, Agent Orange, and the National Memorial. Norman: University of Oklahoma Press, 2004.

U.S. Government   *2007 Essential Guide to Veterans Healthcare*, electronic book on two CD-ROMs. Mt. Laurel, NJ: Progressive Management, 2007.

Jeffrey Wasserman et al.   *An Analysis of Potential Adjustments to the Veterans Equitable Resource Allocation (VERA) System*. Santa Monica, CA: Rand, 2003.

Periodicals

Catherine Arnst   "The Best Medical Care in the US: How Veterans Affairs Transformed Itself—and What It Means to the Rest of Us," *Business Week*, 2006.

S.M. Asch et al.   "Comparison of Quality of Care for Patients in the Veterans Health Administration and Patients in a National Sample," *Annals of Internal Medicine*, December 21, 2004.

Cynthia A. Bascetta   "VA and DOD Health Care," U.S. Government Accounting Office Report GAO-05-1052T, September 28, 2005.

Ari Berman   "Looking Out for Veterans," *Nation*, April 9, 2007.

Greg Bruno   "The Price of Veterans' Health Care," online article sponsored by the Council on Foreign Relations, November 9, 2007.

David F. Burrelli "Military Health Care: The Issue of 'Promised Benefits,'" *CRS Report for Congress*, January 19, 2006.

Bob Filner "Model Healthcare," *Nation*, February 6, 2006.

Sydney J. Freedberg Jr. "Veterans' Health Care Praised, Finally," *National Journal*, February 11, 2006.

Paul Glastris "Political Animal: Best Care Anywhere, . . ." *Washington Monthly*, January 24, 2005.

Thomas Goetz "Physician, Upgrade Thyself," *New York Times*, May 30, 2007.

Rob Hotakainen and Lesley Clark "Health-Care Overhaul Urged for Veterans," *McClatchy Reports*, July 25, 2007.

John Miterko "Congressional Leaders Make Good on Promises to Veterans," *VVA Veteran*, July/August 2007.

Christine M. O'Connell "Walter Reed," *Soldiers*, May 2007.

Nancy Pelosi "President's Budget on Veterans: More of the Same Misplaced Priorities," February 13, 2007. http://majorityleader.house.gov/docUploads/BushBudgetVeterans.pdf.

Jeanine Plant "America's Veterans Left in the Lurch," March 7, 2007. www.alternet.org/rights/48894/.

Toni Reinis

"Military Mental Health Treatment," FDCH Congressional Testimony, May 24, 2007. http://oversight.house.gov/documents/20070524141936.pdf.

Christopher H. Smith

"Veterans' Health Care Fiasco a Long Time Coming," Press Release, March 11, 2007. www.house.gov/list/press/nj04_smith/vahealthcareoped.html.

USA Today

"Military Health Care Woes Extend Beyond Moldy Rooms," March 20, 2007.

Brian Vastag

"Tour of Duty," *Hospitals and Health Networks*, December 2006.

Douglas Waller

"How VA Hospitals Became the Best," *Time*, September 4, 2006.

Matthew C. Wiencke

"Waitless Environment Is Good for Mental Health," *Dartmouth Medicine Magazine*, Summer 2007.

Index